Success in Literacy Reading Tests

UNDERSTANDING
YEAR 6
COMPREHENSION

Excellent for all Students, Teachers, Coaches and Parents

Authors

Alan Horsfield   *M.Ed., B.A., B.Ed., Dip.Sch.Admin., TESOL, Teaching Cert.*
Alan Horsfield has more than 35 years teaching experience in state and private schools in New South Wales and International Schools in Papua New Guinea. He was employed by UNSW (EAA) as an English Research Officer involved in the construction of school tests for English and Mathematics. Alan is a published writer of children's fiction, educational material and school texts.

Elaine Horsfield   *M.A. (Theatre Studies), B.A. (Theatre Media), Teaching Cert.*
Elaine Horsfield has more than 25 years teaching experience in Primary Schools both with the New South Wales Department of Education and in International Schools in Papua New Guinea. She worked with secondary students as coordinator of the NSW Talent Development Project. Elaine is a published writer of children's poetry and educational books.

Understanding Year 6 Comprehension
A. Horsfield © Five Senses Education © W. Marlin

Editor:
Warwick Marlin B.Sc. Dip.Ed.

Publisher:
Five Senses Education
ABN: 16 001 414437
2/195 Prospect Highway
Seven Hills NSW Australia 2147
sevenhills@fivesenseseducation.com.au
www.fivesenseseducation.com.au

Trade Enquiries:
Phone (02) 9838 9265
Fax (02) 9838 8982
Email: fsonline@ fivesenseseducation.com.au

Understanding Year 6 Comprehension
ISBN: 978-1-76032-020-1
1ˢᵗ **Edition:** October 2014
Copyright: Alan Horsfield © Five Senses Education Pty. Ltd. © Warwick Marlin

AUTHOR'S ACKNOWLEDGEMENTS

Warwick Marlin, my editor, whose advice and guidance have been very much appreciated.

Roger Furniss, at Five Senses Education for publishing my books.

And above all, to **Jones**, my typesetter, for a high standard of typesetting, layout and artwork. A very special thank you for your time, patience, attention to detail, and overall quality of your work.

PARENTS

This book tells you what the teacher often does not have the time to explain in detail - the intricacies of a wide variation in text types and the testing strategies used by Australian testing institutions to asses progress in Literacy. It will give you confidence to support your children by reinforcing what is being taught in schools and what is being tested, especially Reading Comprehension.

TEACHERS

This book introduces text types and test question types Australian students should understand to maximise internal and external Reading Tests. Reading tests may involve comprehension as well as related grammar questions. It eliminates the need to wade through lengthy curriculum documents and it provides a clear and easy to follow format for teachers to use. Teachers can also confidently recommend this book to parents as it supports classroom activities and exercises.

B. Ed., Dip. Ed. PRIMARY SCHOOL TEACHERS

This book contains a variety of recognised primary school text types with question sets that will improve reading comprehension and improved results in reading tests. It acts as a quick reference book for teachers in the early years of teaching, when there is so much to learn.

AVAILABILITY OF MATHEMATICS BOOKS

All of the Mathematics books below have been produced by the same editor and publisher, and in many cases the same author (Warwick Marlin). Therefore they all incorporate the same high presentation and philosophy. They can be purchased directly from Five Senses Education, but they are also available in most educational bookshops throughout NSW and Australia (and also some selected bookshops in New Zealand).

New National Curriculum titles

The eight school titles listed directly below have been rewritten and updated in recent years to closely follow the New National Curriculum. **'All levels'** means that the books have been written for students of most ability groups (weak, average and gifted). The graded tests at the end of each chapter ensure that students of most ability groups are extended to their full potential.

❑	YEAR 1	ALL LEVELS
❑	YEAR 2	ALL LEVELS
❑	YEAR 3	ALL LEVELS
❑	YEAR 4	ALL LEVELS
❑	YEAR 5	ALL LEVELS
❑	YEAR 6	ALL LEVELS
❑	YEAR 7	ALL LEVELS
❑	YEAR 8	ALL LEVELS

Other titles in this series

The titles listed below are also available, but they will be fully updated during 2014 and 2015 to also closely follow the new curriculum. However, in the meantime, please note, that these books still adequately address the main features of the new syllabus. We firmly believe that the major topics explained in these titles, and our user friendly presentation and development of the different topics, will always continue to form the vital foundations for all future study and applications of mathematics. This is especially so for the titles up to, and including, Year 10 Advanced.

❑	YEAR 9 & 10	INTERMEDIATE
❑	YEAR 9 & 10	ADVANCED
❑	YEAR 11 & 12	GENERAL MATHS
❑	YEAR 11	EXTENSION 1
❑	YEAR 12	EXTENSION 1

Also by the same Author and Editor (Warwick Marlin)

❑	ESSENTIAL EXERCISES YEAR 1	ALL LEVELS
❑	ESSENTIAL EXERCISES YEAR 2	ALL LEVELS
❑	ESSENTIAL EXERCISES YEAR 3	ALL LEVELS
❑	ESSENTIAL EXERCISES YEAR 4	ALL LEVELS
❑	ESSENTIAL EXERCISES YEAR 5	ALL LEVELS
❑	ESSENTIAL EXERCISES YEAR 6	ALL LEVELS

Developed & written in 2012, this excellent new series of books closely follows the Australian National Curriculum.

CONTENTS

"So it is with children who learn to read fluently and well. They begin to take flight into whole new worlds as effortlessly as young birds take to the sky."

William James

Understanding Year 6 Comprehension
A. Horsfield © Five Senses Education © W. Marlin

UNDERSTANDING YEAR 6 ENGLISH TESTING

For most students this is their last year in primary school. Year 6 is not a NAPLAN testing year. Groundwork commenced and developed in primary years leads to a more formal understanding of literacy and the concepts that contribute to meaning gleaned from the written word. It is a time when the school and the home still work closely together but the child is becoming more independent. It is important that the home maintains a positive attitude to school and education. The move from primary school to high school should be without anxiety. Even though 'homework' will take more and more of the student's time parents still need to provide practical and moral support in an environment that stimulates curiosity and enjoyment of reading and writing. The wider the literacy experiences the child has, the more realistic and practical will be the child's appreciation of the written word in high school years. The student will move through high school years with confidence and ready for new challenges.

Through the final primary year the student will continue to move from literal comprehension of text to the more abstract. What is implied becomes more and more important. Making rational judgments from various texts will be a developing skill. This transition will vary from child to child. At times, we all read different 'messages' into text. It is also important to understand that we don't necessarily grasp the intended meaning on a first reading. Re-reading is an important strategy.

Remember: Do not have unreal expectations of what your child can read. Don't 'push' too hard, especially with the more formal written work. Keep literacy fun, especially in reading and then attitudes will be positive. At times it is fun to read something that is not so challenging!

The best way to succeed in any test is to practice.
An old Chinese proverb sums it up well:

I enjoy a little bit of recreational reading every day!

     I hear, I forget;
     I see, I remember;
     I do, I understand.

The NAPLAN testing program for Australian Schools treats three strands of English.
Reading tests, which include the comprehension of a variety of text types,
Writing tests, which focus on writing a narrative, a persuasive text or a recount,
Language Conventions tests, which include Spelling, Punctuation and Grammar.

All three strands are interrelated in the 'real world'. As the National Curriculum states, "Teaching and learning programs should balance and integrate all three strands" (see:http://www.australiancurriculum.edu.au/Year6).The 'interpretation' of digital text becomes increasingly important and relevant.

This book is based on Year levels not Stages. (There are three basic primary school stages. Year 5 and Year 6 make up Stage 3*. In Year 6 there is a strong emphasis on comprehending a variety of text types of increasing difficulty and subtlety. Not all text types get the same attention. The study of persuasive text is more complex and subtle than, say, following directions. As families and society are a complex mix of differing experiences, children will have different exposure to different text types. Individual children will develop different strengths and weaknesses.

This book focuses specifically on Reading but the skills learned in Reading can assist in the development of the child's Writing skills. The skills learned in the Language Convention strand can improve both Reading and Writing.

That is why we have included a Literacy Tip **(Lit Tip)** component at the end of each set of questions. These may help with any Language Convention questions that come up in standardised reading tests as well adding 'tricks' that may improve the quality of Writing test responses.

*See: http://www.curriculumsupport.education.nsw.gov.au/primary/hsie/teaching/stage3/index.htm

HOW TO USE THIS BOOK EFFECTIVELY

As stated, this book's primary aim is to improve Reading comprehension with some input into Language Conventions. Obviously the Speaking, Listening and Handwriting strands are not included.

The passages are not selected in any specific order but are intended to present a wide variation of text types. Those most likely to be part of the testing situation are treated more often. The text type is shown at the top of each passage as well as in the **List of comprehension passages and exercises** chart that follows.

There will be differences of focus from school to school, as teachers tend to select topics in varying sequences according to their program at a particular time in the year. Some students may also be involved in accelerated promotion, enrichment or remedial activities.

ABOUT THE EXERCISES

The intent of the 40 passages is to provide one passage per week for each school week. This should not impinge too much on obligations set by the school/class teacher for homework and research. There is one easier practice passage provided to make the child aware of a range of question types that may be encountered.
Children need not work through the exercisers from 1 to 40 in the order in which they are presented in this book. There is the option of practicing a particular text type, e.g. poetry.

The Comprehension Answers and the Lit Tip Answers are on separate pages at the back of the book.

Reading texts can be based on either Factual or Literary texts.
Year 6 question types often include the skills of:

- **Locating** such things as information, a sequence of events, literary techniques, grammar conventions and vocabulary features,

- **Identifying** genres, the purpose of a text, literary techniques, appropriate punctuation, word meanings,

- **Interpreting** visual information, multiple pieces of information, language style,

- **Inferring** next events in a text, reasons for a character's action, outcomes, the effect of tense and person, and

- **Synthesising** the tone of a text, the main idea in a text, a character's motivation, the writer's opinion, the intended audience for a text.

These above skills are more or less arranged in an order of difficulty.

Alan Horsfield M.Ed., B.A., B.Ed., Dip.Sch.Admin., TESOL, Teaching Cert.
Elaine Horsfield M. A. (Theatre Studies), B. A. (Theatre Media), Teaching Cert.

TEST SOURCES

The questions, information and practice provided by this book will benefit the student sitting for the following tests.

Externally produced tests

NAPLAN (National Assessment - Literacy and Numeracy) Used Australia wide.
PAT (-R) (Progressive Achievements Tests - Reading)
ICAS (International Competitions and Assessments for Schools) Run by EAA.
Selective Schools and High Schools Placement Tests (Most states have tests specific to that state's educational policy.)
Scholarship Tests
ACER (Australian Council for Educational Research) Scholarship tests (Most states have tests specific to that state's educational policy)
AusVELS (Australian Curriculum in Victoria Essential Learning Standards)
Independent Assessment Agencies (e.g. Academic Assessment Services)
ISA (International Schools Assessment) run by ACER

There may be a number of other independent, external sources for literacy testing.

School produced tests

*   year tests
*   class tests
*   school tests

Information provided in this book may also be beneficial in certain competitions run by commercial enterprises.

A number of commercial publishers also provide books of practice tests.

The purpose of testing

Testing has a variety of purposes and the purpose will often determine the type of test administered. Tests may be used to:
*   determine what the student has learned
*   rank students in order of ability
*   select the most worthy students for a school or class
*   determine the strength and weakness of classroom teaching
*   determine any 'short-comings' in a school's educational program
*   ascertain the effectiveness of certain teaching strategies
*   evaluate the effectiveness of departmental/official syllabuses

The Australian Curriculum (http://www.australiancurriculum.edu.au/Year6) states that Year 6 students should be able to: Identify, describe, and discuss similarities and differences between texts, including those by the same author or illustrator, and evaluate characteristics that define an author's individual style (Examining Literature ACELT1616).
Students should also be able to Identify and explain how choices in language, for example modality, emphasis, repetition and metaphor, influence personal response to different texts (Literature in Context ACELT1615).

A BRIEF SUMMARY OF SOME QUESTION FORMATS

Read the fable by Aesop, **The Fox and the Grapes**, as the text for a set of questions.

A lone fox, lean with hunger, came to a vineyard after much wandering through fields. The vines were rich with fruit, with many bunches of grapes hanging full and ripe, ready for eating.
No one was about so he stole silently in, but upon entering discovered the grapes were high above his head on tall trellises far out of reach.
He jumped but failed to grab the grapes. He tried again and again. All his efforts were in vain. His tired body began to ache after successive jumps to satisfy his hunger. ____(4)____ , frustrated and angry, the fox stumbled back from his last leap and cried out, "I don't want the grapes. They are sour and not fit to eat!" before heading for the hills, like a defeated soldier.

1. Where had the fox been wandering?
   A   past a trellis
   B   through a vineyard
   C   across fields
   D   towards the hills

> Some will take the form of a question: You may have to circle a letter or shade a box.

The question could have been framed so that you have to complete a sentence.

2. When the fox discovered some bunches of grapes he had been wandering
   A   past a trellis   B   through a vineyard
   C   across fields   D   towards the hills

Some questions may have to do with word or phrase meanings.

3. Choose the word that could best replace efforts as used in the text.
   A   attempts   B   leaps   C   achievements   D   work
   (Did you notice the different lay out of the options? They were across the page.)

4. Which word would best go in the space labelled (4)?
   A   Normally   B   Shortly   C   Finally   D   Bravely

5. Write the numbers 1 to 4 in the boxes to show the correct order in which events occurred in the fable. The first one (1) has been done for you.

1	The fox wandered through fields.
	The fox stumbles after his final jump.
	The fox leaves the vineyard and heads for the hills.
	The fox tries many times to snatch the grapes.

> Sometimes you might have to work out the sequence in which events occurred.

Some questions are called *free response questions*. You will have to write an answer.

6. What were the grapes hanging from? Write your answer on the line? _____

Sometimes you might have to decide if something is TRUE or FALSE.

7. Tick the box to show if this statement is TRUE or FALSE.
   The grapes hanging from the trellis were not ripe.   TRUE ☐   FALSE ☐

There will be times when you will have to read the whole text and make a judgement.

8. What point does the fable portray?
   A   time solves all difficult problems   B   one good turn deserves another
   C   people find excuses for their failure   D   pride comes before a fall

9. There might be a question about the use of language in the text.
   The phrase: *like a defeated soldier* (last line), is an example of a
   A   metaphor   B   simile

10. You might have to decide if, according to the text, a statement is FACT or OPINION.
   Are the fox's words, "They are sour and not fit to eat", a fact or an opinion? _____

Answers: 1. C, 2. C, 3. A, 4. C, 5. (1, 3, 4, 2), 6. trellises, 7. FALSE, 8. C, 9. B (metaphor) 10. opinion

Understanding Year 6 Comprehension
A. Horsfield © Five Senses Education © W. Marlin

This is a practice page. (The answers follow the questions)

Read the report *Triple Letter Words.*

Triple Letter Words

We often see double letters in words. Examples include abbey, putting, broom, taxiing, powwow. In fact, there is an example of a word with a double for virtually every letter of the alphabet. If we included surnames or foreign words that are now entering the English language we might find every letter can be used as a double.

Triple letter words are a rarity in dictionaries. They are less accepted now-a-days than they have been in the past because the usual conventions of formal English spelling disallow triple letters. We put hyphens in words that contain three of the same letters <u>in a row</u> to break up the series of letters, e.g. bee-eater (a small bird), *bell-like, cross-section, joss-stick,* and *shell-less.*

Alternatively, the trend is to drop one of the letters from the triple. A person who flees is a *fleer*, not a *fleeer* (flee + er) and someone who sees is a *seer*, not a *seeer* (see + er). Chaffinches used to be called *chaff finches*, but when the two words were merged, one *f* was dropped.

Another problem arises as to which dictionary is the most up to date - or trusted. A triple letter word may be, or may have once been, in one dictionary but not in another. Does this discrepancy mean that the 'word' is not a word?

There are triple letter words that have appeared in at least one English dictionary, usually as an old spelling or rare variation. Examples include frillless, stewardessship, brrr, and yayyy. The last two are sometimes referred to as representation of noises and don't count. If this is the case then words such as clang and boom could be suspect words? I don't think so!

However, in the world of advertising and in such publications as graphic novels and magazines one will often find these 'words': brrr, shhh, vrooom, hmmm, haaa and zzz. Many are often extended to quadruple letter (or more) words. *Vroooom* makes a stronger point than *vrooom*. A zzzzzz sleep is a much deeper sleep than a zzz sleep!

It would be great if triple letter words were _____(8)_____ .

Understanding Reports   Circle a letter or write an answer for questions 1 to 8.

1. What purpose does a hyphen (-) serve in triple letter words?
    A   it highlights a defect in modern dictionaries
    B   it shows how to form the compound word
    C   it makes them more readily interpreted
    D   it prevents spelling mistakes

2. Triple letter words have never been accepted in dictionaries.
Is this statement TRUE or FALSE?
Tick a box.
             TRUE ☐   FALSE ☐

3. What would be a suitable replacement for *in a row* as used in paragraph 2?
    A   in order   B   in succession
    C   in line   D   in a queue

4. This text is most likely intended to
    A   entertain the reader regarding oddities in English
    B   teach the reader to spell multi-lettered words
    C   warn the reader about the reliability of dictionaries
    D   persuade the reader to buy a new dictionary

5. Which of these options from the text is an opinion and not a fact?
    A   It would be great if triple letter words were more acceptable.
    B   In fact, many are often extended to quadruple letter (or more) words.
    C   We often see double letters in words.
    D   Triple letter words are a rarity in dictionaries.

6. Which statement best reflects the writer's attitude to triple letter words?
    A   Triple letter words should be removed from dictionaries.
    B   Triple letter words serve no useful purpose in modern times.
    C   Triple letter words should only be used to represent noises.
    D   Triple letter words play an important part in written communications.

7. The letters *grrr* are representing a feeling of
    A   hostility   B   approval   C   friendship   D   confusion

8. Words have been deleted from the last line of the text.
Which words would be best suited to the opinion expressed in the text for the space (8)?
    A   forever banned
    B   more accepted
    C   only used in advertising
    D   removed from dictionaries

Answers: 1. C   2. FALSE   3. B   4. A   5. A   6. D   7. A   8. B

Understanding Year 6 Comprehension
A. Horsfield © Five Senses Education © W. Marlin

Year 6 Comprehension Passages and Exercises

Each of the 40 passages has a set of eight questions – comprehension and language questions, based upon that text. Following the questions is a section called **Lit Tip** (short for Literacy Tips). These are gems of information that are intended to develop the child's responses to Language Conventions questions arising in texts and tests. They may also be beneficial when answering questions in Language Convention (Grammar) papers or when completing Writing assessment tasks.

Understanding Year 6 Comprehension
A. Horsfield © Five Senses Education © W. Marlin

1 Read the narrative extract *Cat v Plant.*

Note: a sundew is a small carniverous plant that traps very small insects for nutrition. Now read on.

Cat v Plant

Within a week Lorenzo's sundew had several more new, green traps as big as a large coin — and was starting to catch bigger insects. One day it must have caught a butterfly. There were butterfly wings on the cobblestones.

Briefly Lorenzo wondered if he might have done something wrong.

Lorenzo decided to stop feeding it plant food, but he would have to get a bigger pot.

He found a large green tub and got some potting mix from under the counter of his mother's garden shop. It was called Rapid Growth Plus.

By the end of a month the Fly Traps were almost as big as a small hand — and getting bigger!

If Lorenzo quickly touched the open jaws with the tip of his finger, they snapped shut so fast he could hardly see them move. He made sure he pulled his hand away quickly.

Each fine morning he would drag his plant out into the sunny corner in the front of the shop. Each afternoon he would drag it back into his mother's shop. It was too big to take upstairs.

'Glad they don't eat people,' his father had joked as he left for work one morning.

That thought had crossed Lorenzo's mind. He didn't like the idea.

Then late one afternoon he saw Gladiator, Mrs Bellini's horrid cat, sneaking up on his plant. Lorenzo watched from inside the shop door.

Gladiator was stalking his plant!

Suddenly he sprung and swiped at the plant with his open claw. The plant pulled back — shocked.

Then to Lorenzo's amazement the plant struck back. It's open trap just missing the cat's whiskers.

Gladiator pulled back in shock. His back arched and the hairs on his neck stood straight up. Then he crouched down low like a leopard stalking its prey. He wasn't going to be threatened by a plant!

Lorenzo rushed outside, shouting at the cat.

Understanding Narratives

Circle a letter to answer questions 1 to 8.

1. A carnivorous plant is one that
    - A   is dependent upon sunlight for survival
    - B   is carried from one site to another
    - C   eats creatures for its survival
    - D   quickly outgrows its pot

2. Lorenzo's sundew was growing rapidly because
    - A   he had it growing in a large green pot
    - B   he planted it in rich potting mix
    - C   it was put in the sunlight each day
    - D   it caught many insects to eat

3. Which word best describes how Lorenzo felt about his plant? He was
    - A   disinterested
    - B   fearful
    - C   neglectful
    - D   protective

4. What thought crossed Lorenzo's mind that worried him?
    - A   Gladiator was going to eat his plant.
    - B   The green pot was too big to drag outside.
    - C   The sundew might eat people.
    - D   His sundew was not getting enough food.

5. Which of the following options from the text is a simile?
    - A   he crouched down low like a leopard stalking its prey
    - B   Lorenzo wondered if he might have done something wrong
    - C   it was too big to take upstairs
    - D   they snapped shut so fast he could hardly see them move

6. Which word from the first paragraph is not a compound word?
    - A   sundew
    - B   butterfly
    - C   insects
    - D   cobblestones

7. How would Gladiator be best described?
    - A   meek
    - B   agressive
    - C   inquisitive
    - D   sluggish

8. What happened to the sundew when Gladiator attacked it?
    - A   it avoided the onslaught
    - B   it had its traps damaged
    - C   it wilted after the attack
    - D   it became very distressed

Need to try another narrative? Check the contents page.

Lit Tip 1 – Improve your Literacy skills   Plurals for names from initials

Many things are refered to by their initials, e.g. ATM for Automatic Teller Machine.
How do we refer to the plural form of ATM. Many people add an apostrophe s ('s).
This is wrong. The correct form is ATMs. The s is a lower case s.
Examples: DVDs, 1900s, SUVs (sports utility vehicles), POWs (prisoners of war), 4WDs

Choose the correct option to complete this sentence.
Dave needed a computer so he checked out _____ in the local paper.
    - A   pc's
    - B   PCs
    - C   PC's
    - D   PCS

Understanding Year 6 Comprehension
A. Horsfield © Five Senses Education © W. Marlin

2 Read the movie poster *The Blob.*

The Blob

Film posters are used to advertise a film. They normally contain an image with text. Prior to the 1990s, illustrations from the film, instead of photos of stars, were more common. The text on a poster usually contains the film title in large lettering and the names of the main actors. It may also include the name of the director, names of characters and the release date.

The original version of The Blob was made in 1958. It depicts a growing protoplasm-like alien creature that came from outer space and terrorised the small town of Downingtown. There have been subsequent remakes.

Understanding Persuasions

Circle a letter to answer questions 1 to 8.

1. The poster is attempting to attract viewers who would enjoy
    - A   horror movies
    - B   comedies
    - C   romance movies
    - D   fantasies

2. Who is most likely the star of the film?
    - A   Aneta Corseau
    - B   Kate Phillips
    - C   Steve McQueen
    - D   Earl Rowe

3. Which part of the poster dominates the poster?
    - A   the name of the film
    - B   the name of the star actor
    - C   a graphic from the film
    - D   the faces of the characters

4. The words *indestructible* and *indescribable* as used on the poster are
    - A   nouns
    - B   adjectives
    - C   adverbs
    - D   verbs

5. The monster as portrayed on the poster, is most likely, a
    - A   a robotic monster
    - B   super-intelligent alien
    - C   a mythical beast
    - D   shapeless living organism

6. What feature was more important on film posters after the 1990s?
    - A   a succinct descriptions of the film's plot
    - B   the release date of the film to cinemas
    - C   photos of the stars in the movie
    - D   large dominating reproduction of the film's title

7. The expression on the faces on the poster show
    - A   awe
    - B   amazement
    - C   excitement
    - D   terror

8. The word *subsequent* as used in the second introductory paragraph of text means a
    - A   production coming after the original movie
    - B   movie of lower quality than the original
    - C   remake that is more successful than previous versions
    - D   sequel to the original movie

Need to try another persuasive text? Check the contents page.

Lit Tip 2 – Improve your literacy skills   **Better words than went**

It is easy to overuse the *went* type words in story writing. More precise words are available which can improve your story.

Look at these three examples:
1. Jan <u>went</u> home.   2. Jan <u>hurried</u> home.   3. Jan <u>strolled</u> home.
Examples 2 and 3 give the reader some insight into how Jan went home.
Here are some other options: trudged, sprinted, stumbled, danced, bounded, plodded.

Find three better words than *walked* that help readers get a more precise picture.
Patty *walked* towards the water.
1._____   2. _____   3. _____

Understanding Year 6 Comprehension
A. Horsfield © Five Senses Education © W. Marlin

Read the description *Paperbark Creek.*

Paperbark Creek

Paperbark Creek was so small a settlement that you could almost see all of it from the top veranda of The Mariner's Hotel. To the left was a road, surprisingly called The Boulevard, which followed the creek line north to where the creek entered the sea. Not much moved along the street. The road was relatively even and unbroken for two kilometres until it degenerated into a series of deep, dusty ruts and furrows as it edged towards the sand dune, where the few visitors were rewarded to the back view of what was once a public toilet complex.

In the northerly direction from the hotel lay all the amenities of the village — the two-roomed schoolhouse, a weatherboard hall that sometimes doubled as a church, a house that was advertised on a flaky sign as a B&B — bed and breakfast, and a general store that looked like it had discovered the place many years ago and had squatted there.

This end of Paperbark Creek, looked much the same as many other coastal villages—quiet, dry and unexciting—and likely to stay that way until some developer discovered its unspoilt nature and got permission, and the money, to put in a subdivision—or even a proper camping ground. So far this sort of development had not come to Paperbark Creek. Kombi vans were the surfers' choice of accommodation.

Paperbark Creek was a magnet for small groups of surfers avoiding the more popular spots further up the coast. A number of retirees lived in town. Their reason for living there was as much to do with fishing as to do with their meagre pensions.

To the south, the village was hemmed by a steep rocky slope rising up from the creek, on one side of the road. On the seawardside was a paperbark wetland, often dry, but could be covered in floodwater for a week if rain persisted.

And there was a cross by the roadside.

Understanding Descriptions   Circle a letter or write an answer for questions 1 to 8.

1. Which word best describes the village of Paperbark Creek?

    A   flourishing   B   sleepy   C   morbid   D   inspiring

2. Who were the main visitors to Paperbark Creek?

    A   tourists   B   retirees
    C   fisherpersons   D   surfboard riders

3. The wetland was to the north of The Mariner's Hotel.

    Is this statement TRUE or FALSE? Tick a box.   TRUE ☐   FALSE ☐

4. The narrator states: a road, surprisingly called The Boulevard in paragraph 1.
   Why is he surprised by the name Boulevard?

    A   the road is very unlike a boulevard
    B   it is a word with a foreign origin being used in Australia
    C   there were no trees in Paperbark Creek
    D   the narrator didn't know boulevard was a real name

5. What does the cross by the roadside suggest?

    A   It advertises a church service in the local hall.
    B   A motor fatality had happened at that spot.
    C   The cross is a warning to motorists to slow down.
    D   It indicated the entrance to the local cemetery.

6. According to the text, which statement is CORRECT?

    A   Visiting surfers preferred to stay in the hotel.
    B   The camping ground was next to the motel.
    C   Most of the village was to the north of the hotel.
    D   Paperbark Creek had a new general store.

7. The text implies that the public toilet complex

    A   was well maintained   B   was under repairs
    C   had been vandalised   D   had fallen into disuse

8. The narrator feels any new development in the village is

    A   doubtful   B   impossible   C   probable   D   imminent

Need to try another description? Check the contents page.

Understanding Year 6 Comprehension
A. Horsfield © Five Senses Education © W. Marlin

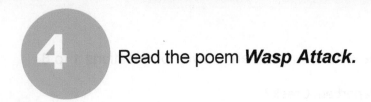

4 Read the poem *Wasp Attack.*

Wasp Attack

As colour leaves the trees

and returns to the lawn

wasps circle, nonchalant

waiting for traffic to clear

from the bunker

in the stump's soft centre

I stoop to sabotage the nest

at the rear-guard blitz I stagger back

in frenzied batting at wasps

tangling my hair, clothes-crawling

stinging me over and under

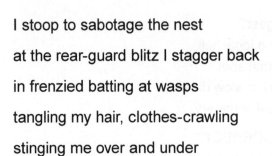

At dusk when the wasps have clocked in

I don battle gear and spray revenge

in dense white powder

The garden is mine again

Jennifer Chrystie

Source: My thanks to Jennifer Chrystie for giving permission to include this poem from her book *Weight of Snow*
published 2013 p.59

Understanding Poetry

Circle a letter or write an answer for questions 1 to 8.

1. What did the narrator initially intend doing?
   She intended to

A	watch colour fall from the trees	B	put on army-style clothes
C	hunt wasps from her garden	D	remove soft tree stumps

2. What word does the poet use to mean put on (clothes)?
   Write your answer on the line. _____

3. What is the meaning of the word bunker as used in the poem?

A	a nesting hive for wasps	B	an underground shelter
C	a sand filled dip on a golf course	D	a place to store garden refuse

4. What was the wasps' reaction to the narrator's first attack on the wasps' nest?
   A   They fled from the garden.
   B   They went deeper into the stump.
   C   They retreated until they could reform.
   D   They attacked the narrator in droves.

5. The narrator 'defeated' the wasps by

A	poisoning them at dusk	B	destroying their nest
C	covering the nest in leaves	D	sabotaging the nest

6. When the narrator first sees the wasps they are

A	returning to their nest	B	becoming agitated
C	calm and relaxed	D	preparing to attack

7. The poet mainly uses images associated with
   A   work   B   gardens   C   deciduous trees   D   warfare

8. What word would describe the narrator's second attack on the wasps?
   A   merciful   B   tentative   C   calculated   D   brazen

Need to try another poem? Check the contents page.

Lit Tip 4 – Improve your Literacy skills   Poetry or prose

Prose is the common form of written (and spoken) language that doesn't have a metrical structure, that is, it doesn't have a set or consistent rhythm.

Poetry is a rhythmical composition written (or spoken) that provides pleasure through the use of imaginative language. It does not have to rhyme. Blank verse does not rhyme.
Some prose has a very strong poetic quality, such as the speech of orators.

A script is usually a written text for another media (film/play). It may include stage directions as well as words spoken by actors.

Is the poem, 'Wasp Attack' an example of blank verse?   Yes ☐   No ☐

Understanding Year 6 Comprehension
A. Horsfield © Five Senses Education © W. Marlin

What is Art Deco?

The style now called Art Deco originated in Europe in the early years of the 20th Century. It had its heyday from 1920 to 1940. Art Deco expressed all the vigour and optimism of the 'roaring' twenties (1920s) and the idealism and escapism of the depressions after WWI and the early 1930s. It represented the ideals of streamlining, and the importance of invention using geometrical shapes. Buildings of the era had a very distinctive style.

Here are some of the symbols from one of the world's great Art Deco cities — Napier in New Zealand.

The The use of geometric shapes including V-shaped stripes, circles and triangles representing machines and technology that people thought would solve society's problems.

Symbols of **energy, power** and **technology** with new developments in transport and communications.

The **zig-zag** which was associated with radio and electric waves, lightning bolts and man-made patterns.

Art Deco was not restricted to New Zealand. New York gained a world-wide reputation for skyscrapers in the 1920s–1930s.

The shape of the **skyscraper** — a symbol of the early 20th Century.

Adapted from:
Art Deco Motifs in Napier
http://en.wikipedia.org/wiki/Art_Deco

Sun bursts and fountains were used to represent the dawn of a new era.

Understanding Explanations   Circle a letter or write an answer for questions 1 to 8.

1. The Art Deco period produced a feeling of

  A   optimism   B   confusion   C   apathy   D   neglect

2. This is a V-shaped stripe seen around the exterior of an Art Deco building.
It is intended to represent

  A   advances in energy and power
  B   machines and technology
  C   the dawn of a new era
  D   the coming of skyscrapers

3. Which symbol was used to represent radio and electric waves?

  A   sun bursts   B   straight lines
  C   the zig-zag   D   transport

4. What is most likely implied by the word *roaring* as used in paragraph 1?

  A   burning fiercely   B   producing growling sounds
  C   getting very angry   D   exciting times

5. Art Deco had its heyday (paragraph 1) in the 1920s and 1930s.
A heyday is

  A   the season's end when crops are harvested
  B   the one day when everyone is happy
  C   a period of great success
  D   the time between wars or depressions

6. People living in the 1920s and 1930s would have believed that

  A   the world was going to be a better place
  B   the limits of achievement had been reached
  C   there would never be another world war
  D   change takes a long time to happen

7. Which word in paragraph 1 relates to making machines and buildings that are efficient and operate smoothly?
Write your answer on the line. _____

8. Which word best describes the designs of Art Deco buildings?

  A   functional   B   extravagant   C   simplistic   D   decorative

Need to try another explanation? Check the contents page.

Lit Tip 5 – Improve your Literacy skills   **The ampersand (&)**

The ampersand symbol (&) should only be used in informal writing such as emails, tweets, memos and in quickly taken notes. Sometimes the ampersand can be used in titles if space is limited, in signs or where the ampersand is part of a business brand name or common usage. Use the word *and,* **not** ampersands in text.

Circle the best option to complete these sentences.
1. Aman (and, &) his son walked to the shop.   3. We saw a Cobb (and, &) Co. coach.
2. I stayed overnight in McAdam's B (and, &) B*.   (* Bed - Breakfast)

Read the procedure *How to Grow Sprouts.*

How to Grow Sprouts

Sprouts are the first growth of a seed. They are like the first little pops of green that speckle the fresh ground in the garden.

Sprouts are delicious treats grown at home. With a small number of ingredients and simple steps anyone can grow their own microgreens.

Getting started

When purchasing seeds make sure that they are marked "sprouting" seeds.

The equipment is simple

- plastic or glass tray with a large flat base

- fine mesh or gauze

- stainless steel strainer

1. Soak the seeds overnight

In the evening pour a generous layer of sprout seeds into the bottom of the tray. Cover with about 2 centimetres of non-chlorinated water. Swirl the seeds, drain, and then cover again with water. Cover the tray with a piece of protective mesh. Leave the tray on the bench top over night.

2. Drain the seeds

The next morning drain off the water. Repeat the process of rinsing, swirling, and draining. Use the strainer to prevent loss of seeds. Add water to the tray and let stand.

3. Continue rinsing and draining

Two to three times per day swirl, drain well, and replace the water. Every day the sprouts will grow a little until they have filled the entire tray and started to turn green. It may take 3 to 5 days.

4. Store spouts

When satisfied with the length and greenness of the sprouts, they are ready to be stored in the refrigerator. The sprouts need to be as dry as possible. Keeping them dry will stop their growth and slow down spoilage. Sprouts usually keep for six days.

5. Eat sprouts!

Sprouts are great on sandwiches, mixed with greens in salads, in stir-fries or as a crunchy snack. Whereas the seed would be difficult to digest, the new sprout turns into a nourishing plant food. Different seeds have different flavoured sprouts.

Understanding Procedures   Circle a letter or write an answer for questions 1 to 8.

1. This information on growing sprouts would be most appropriate for
    A   a backyard gardener   B   children with a weight problem
    C   people living in flats   D   chefs providing vegetarian meals

2. Sprouts are called microgreens. This suggests that sprouts are
    A   a very light green in colour B   mini salad vegetables
    C   only suitable for snacks   D   too small to be easily seen

3. According to the text about how long will dried sprouts keep in the fridge?
    A   3 days   B   4 days   C   5 days   D   6 days

4. The main advantage in growing sprouts is that they
    A   can be grown in the kitchen   B   use chlorine-free water
    C   are fresh when harvested   D   do not require any attention

5. Write the numbers 1 to 4 in the boxes to show the correct order in which events occurred in the procedure. The first one (1) has been done for you.

☐	rinse seeds in clean water
☐	soak seeds in water overnight
☐	drain water from seed tray
1	buy seeds that are marked "sprouting" seeds

6. Step 5, **Eat sprouts!** has an exclamation mark.
    What is the writer trying to tell the reader by using the exclamation mark.
    A   the sprouts may not be ready for eating
    B   don't eat all the sprouts at once
    C   treat the sprouts carefully
    D   now is the time to enjoy the sprouts

7. Which option from the text is a simile?
    A   as dry as possible   B   seeds have different flavoured sprouts
    C   like the first little pops of green   D   every day the sprouts will grow a little

8. Which option best describes how the writer feels about growing sprouts?
    A   enthusiastic   B   reserved   C   speechless   D   doubtful

Need to try another procedure? Check the contents page.

Lit Tip 6 – Improve your Literacy skills   What is idiom?

Idiom is a saying that has a meaning that is not obvious from the literal meaning. We all use idiom and usually know what it means. Don't use it in formal writing!

When we say, "Joe has green fingers," We are not talking about the colour of Joe's fingers but his gardening ability. We are actually saying, "Joe is a very good gardener."
She'll be apples means *everything will be OK*. Nothing to do with apples!

What reaction does the idiom, *stone the crows*, suggest?_____

Understanding Year 6 Comprehension
A. Horsfield © Five Senses Education © W. Marlin

Families Connected?

With ample access to mass communications are we really connecting more with other human beings? I don't think so.

It seems that everyone is spending more time at work, studying or alone, and less time with their families and friends. People are busier, or at least more occupied, than ever before!

In the past the father worked a set number of hours a week and the mother stayed at home doing domestic work, taking care of children, shopping for food, cooking and cleaning. Now both parents might work. They have to share the shopping, cooking and cleaning in their free time. Parents don't have as much time with their children as they had in the past. They spend less time with their friends and neighbours.

There are now more single parent families. The single parent has to do everything. These days, many school age children come home from school to an empty home. Many children spend hours in front of the television or playing with hand-held devices. Even when families are together, it is common for members to do things by themselves. For example, they watch programs on separate TVs in different rooms, they use the Internet and they talk or text with friends on their mobile phones. Many parents bring work home. They sit in front of their computers at night.

Often families watch television while eating a meal. There is very little real talk.

Isn't it strange? Thanks to technology, people are able to communicate so easily with people all over the world, but are they saying anything important? Often these people don't communicate as well as before even with people in their own homes!

Do you think I am right?

Adapted from: an idea in Side by Side (3rd Ed) S. J Molinski and B Bliss, Longmans 2001.

Understanding Opinions

Circle a letter to answers questions 1 to 8.

1. According to the writer, modern communication
   A   can only get better
   B   encourages people to be lazy
   C   is too reliant on technology
   D   has improved with technology

2. The writer adds a question mark to the title to
   A   suggest that families are not better connected
   B   involve the reader in a controversy
   C   enlist the reader's support for the opinion expressed
   D   give an example of poor communication skills

3. What is one important advantage of modern communication technology?
   A   communication devices are now hand-held
   B   people are now able to communicate with more people
   C   parents need not be interrupted while they are working
   D   television sets can be located in any room of the house

4. What reason does the writer give for less talk between family members?
   A   families are more interested in playing games
   B   there is more involvement with their friends and neighbours
   C   shopping and housework are more time consuming
   D   both parents have heavy workloads

5. The writer states that family members do things by themselves.
   The words, *by themselves*, could be replaced with the word
   A   personally   B   individually   C   secretly   D   privately

6. What is the common term for domestic work as used in paragraph 3?
   A   homework   B   handiwork   C   housework   D   clockwork

7. The writer feels that the quality of modern communication is
   A   deteriorating   B   abysmal   C   practical   D   inspiring

8. According to the text, single parents
   A   need help with the family shopping   B   live in empty homes
   C   leave their children unsupervised   D   have less time with their children

Need to try another opinion/persuasive text? Check the contents page.

Lit Tip 7 – Improve your literacy skills   Rhetorical questions

When we ask a question we usually expect an answer. There are situations where you don't really expect an answer. Such questions are called **rhetorical questions.**

Have you heard someone say, "Well, how about that?" They don't expect an answer to this question. They are drawing attention to something that is unusual or odd.

Text 7 ends with a rhetorical question. It is meant to make the reader think about the problem and form an opinion. Rhetorical questions are a clever technique to use in persuasive writing but don't use them too often.

Underline a rhetorical question in the second last paragraph.

Understanding Year 6 Comprehension
A. Horsfield © Five Senses Education © W. Marlin

8 Read the recount *Lombok Floating Palace.*

Lombok Floating Palace

Located in the town of Cakranegara, the Mayura Garden has a very old structure that was built by ancient Balinese who settled on the Lombok Island near Bali (Indonesia).

When the Balinese people decided to build a kingdom on Lombok, they built picturesque temples and palaces. The Mayura Garden used to be a part of one those palaces. This beautiful water palace consists of a large artificial lake with a 'floating' pavilion connected to the shoreline by a raised footpath. It was used as a meeting place and court of justice during the reign of the Balinese in the kingdom of Lombok.

Also called the Floating Temple or Mayura Water Palace, it was built around 1744. It was one of the construction projects of the Balinese Raja (King). The Raja was excited by the opportunity to develop the newly discovered island, and constructed buildings that rivalled the nearby kingdom in Bali. The vast water garden was one of the Rajah's masterpieces. The 'floating' hall was used as the hall of justice and a meeting place for important state gatherings or religious events. The architectural style within the complex was clearly influenced by a blending of Hindu and Islamic styles. The spaciousness of the garden courts is similar to the palaces found in Central Java.

The Mayura Garden has a row of mangosteen fruit trees. The shallow, man-made lake is full of lotus plants. Inside the pavilion are ancient statues of Muslim and Hindu characters and in the surrounding area are the remains of an old Hindu temple. Mayura Garden reminds local people of the time when Islam was bought to Lombok by Arabian, Chinese and Makassar people. Now people of different races live comfortably side by side respecting their differences.

The site lost its splendour and its functions shortly after the Dutch took control of the Indonesian islands. Today, one can only imagine what this palace once looked like but the park is still enjoyed by the local people.

Photo: A. Horsfield

Understanding Recounts

Circle a letter or write an answer for questions 1 to 8.

1. What played an important part in the architectural design of the floating palace?
    - A its location and the availability of the water
    - B the proximity of a row of mangosteen fruit trees
    - C the beauty of the surrounding Mayura Garden
    - D a blending of Hindu and Islamic styles

2. The Lombok Palace in the town of Cakranegara really floats on water.
   Is this likely to be TRUE or FALSE?

   Tick a box   TRUE ☐   FALSE ☐

3. Because the people of Lombok are of many religions they have become
    - A suspicious of one another
    - B concerned about their rights
    - C aggressive in their beliefs
    - D tolerant of the beliefs of others

4. What happened to the floating palace when the Dutch took over Indonesia?
    - A it was abandoned
    - B it fell into disrepair
    - C it was used as a Dutch palace
    - D it was given back to the Balinese

5. To get from the Mayura Garden to the palace people have to
    - A go by small boat
    - B cross over using a bridge
    - C walk along a raised walkway
    - D wade through the water

6. Write the numbers 1 to 4 in the boxes to show the correct order in which events occurred in the recount. The first one (1) has been done for you.

   ☐ the floating palace was built around 1744
   ☐ the Dutch take control of the Indonesian islands
   ☐ important people use the palace for religious events
   ☐ 1 ☐ the ancient Balinese people settle on Lombok Island

7. A visitor to the Mayura Garden would find the place
    - A busy
    - B peaceful
    - C eerie
    - D exciting

8. Where do the lotus plants grow?
    - A in the water around the palace
    - B in the remains of an old Hindu temple
    - C under the mangosteen fruit trees
    - D inside the pavilion near ancient statues

Need to try another recount? Check the contents page.

Lit Tip 8 – Improve your Literacy skills   **The suffix *ship***

Suffixes are letters added to the end of base words to modify their meaning.
Example: to change many verbs to past tense we add *ed*: walk - walked
Ship can be a suffix. It indicates a quality (friendship), a skill (leadership), a status (citizenship) or a 'collection' (membership).
Two people can form a partnership. Partnership is **not** a compound word.

1. A contest to find a champion is a _____ event.
2. People in the same town live in a _____.
3. When people own something they have _____ of that thing.

Understanding Year 6 Comprehension
A. Horsfield © Five Senses Education © W. Marlin

Vietnamese Rice Legend

(Note: A legend is a traditional story sometimes regarded as historical but cannot be authenticated.)

According to the legend the gods did not mean for humankind to labour so intensively in cultivating rice. In fact, rice was supposed to grow naturally, effortlessly, and abundantly. It was not meant to be farmed.

The gods sent a messenger spirit to bring rice to humankind. He carried two magical seed pouches, each containing a different variety of seed. The first one held seeds that would grow as soon as they hit the ground and would provide a bountiful harvest without the need for cultivation. However the second pouch held seeds that would require work, but it would make the land appear beautiful if given proper care.

Now, the gods intended for the first seeds to become rice, while the second should be grass. The rice would provide plenty of nutrition to all, while the grass would cover the land and make the earth more habitable and picturesque. The messenger got the two pouches confused, and this caused great hardship for the humans! Rice was extremely difficult to grow, demanding months of back-breaking labour and attention, while the grass freely grew everywhere.

At this point, the gods became angry and kicked the faulted messenger spirit out of the heavens. They sent him down to earth in the form of a beetle, made to scurry around in the grass where he would have to dodge the steps of wandering humans.

But the trouble didn't end there. The legend goes on to say, the gods meant to help humankind. So they ordered the rice to ball itself up and present itself in convenient rolls to humans so that they might collect it more easily for cooking.

Obediently, the rice balls rolled into the very first house in the first village. Shocked by the sight, the lady of the house struck the rice balls with her broom, flinging the grains of rice in a thousand directions. Angry and skulking, the rice took to the fields and spurned humans. As it is to this day, men and women must go to the fields to cultivate rice. It is a difficult and time-consuming trade, but it provides the world with a great source of nutrition.

Adapted from: http://contrau.wordpress.com/2010/11/01/vietnamese_folk_tale/

Understanding Legends

Circle a letter or write an answer for questions 1 to 8.

1. This legend explains
   - A   how to cultivate rice
   - B   the importance of rice as a food
   - C   where to grow the best rice
   - D   how rice agriculture began

2. How was the spirit messenger punished for his mistake?
   - A   He was turned into a rice ball.
   - B   He was struck with a broom.
   - C   He was changed into a beetle to live in the grass.
   - D   He was forced to labour in the rice fields.

3. How many attempts did the gods make to help humankind?

   Write your answer in the box. ☐

4. The seeds in the messenger's second pouch were intended to
   - A   make the world picturesque
   - B   provide a shelter for beetles
   - C   give families a nutritious crop
   - D   save farmers from heavy labour

5. When the lady of the house saw the rice ball enter her house she
   - A   knew it was a gift from the gods
   - B   saved the seeds for planting in the field
   - C   struck it with her broom
   - D   understood a mistake had been made

6. What is the meaning of the word *wandering* as used in paragraph 4?
   - A   exploring
   - B   roaming
   - C   trespassing
   - D   scurrying

7. The word *work* as used in paragraph 2 is a
   - A   verb
   - B   adjective
   - C   noun
   - D   adverb

8. What part of this legend is most likely to be true?
   - A   a messenger brought the seed to earth
   - B   the rice ball was annoyed for being struck
   - C   the gods gave the messenger two types of seed
   - D   rice requires a lot of hard work to grow

Need to try another legend? Check the contents page.

Lit Tip 9 – Improve your Literacy skills   **Noun or verb?**

Some words can be nouns or verbs (or even other parts of speech) depending upon the context - the sentence they are used in. Look at *drive* in these two sentences.

1. Mum can *drive* a truck. (verb)   **2.** We went for a long *drive* into the hills. (noun)
(drive here is an action word)   (drive here is the name of an activity)

Nouns are often preceded by an article or adjective.
Write V (verb) or N (noun) to show the part of speech of the underlined word.
1. I can <u>post</u> the letter. ( )   The letter is in the <u>post</u> .( )
2. Will Ron <u>ring</u> your mother? ( )   Dan drew a <u>ring</u> around the square. ( )
3. The <u>radio</u> was switched on. ( )   We must <u>radio</u> the shore for help. ( )

Understanding Year 6 Comprehension
A. Horsfield © Five Senses Education © W. Marlin

10 Read the text and diagram for *The Eather Family tree.*

The Eather Family Tree

A family tree, or pedigree chart, is a chart representing family relationships in a conventional tree structure.

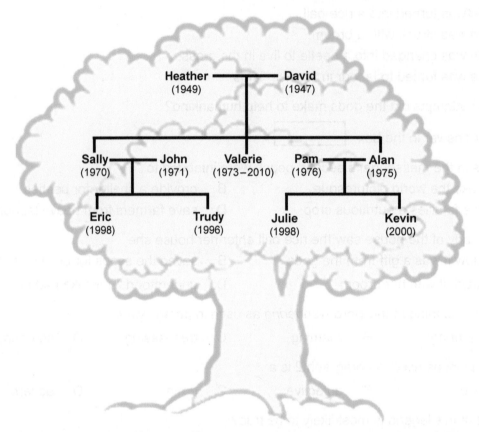

This diagram is of the Eather family tree. All the members of the Eather family are represented—parents, children, grandparents, grandchildren, aunts, uncles, cousins, nieces and nephews. There are two types of relations. Those related by marriage and those related by birth, which are often referred to as blood relations.

Family trees show who is married and who is not. It also shows the children of married couples. Heather and David are the parents of Sally, Valerie and Alan.

Here are some relationships revealed by the Eather family tree.

A cousin is a relative with whom a person shares one or more common ancestors.

Eric and Kevin are cousins because they are the sons of siblings. Sibling is the name given to children of the same parents. John is Julie and Kevin's uncle. Sally is their aunt.

This family tree does not show when people got married.

Adapted from: an idea in Side by Side, Book 2 by S J Molinski and B Bliss 2002
http://en.wikipedia.org/wiki/Family_tree
http://www.thefreedictionary.com/blood+relationship

Understanding Family Trees

Circle a letter or write an answer for questions 1 to 8.

1. How many generations does the Eather family tree show?

   A   1   B   3

   C   4   D   11

2. Who is married to Alan?

   A   Pam   B   Valerie

   C   Sally   D   Julie

A sign reads: *Families are like trees - the branches may grow in different directions but the roots are the same*

3. These dates (1973–2010) are under Valerie's name.
   These dates represent when Valerie was born and when she

   A   got married   B   had children

   C   left home   D   died

4. Who is the oldest of Heather and David's grandchildren?

   A   Eric   B   Trudy   C   Julie   D   Kevin

5. How many cousins does Trudy have?

   A   1   B   2

   C   3   D   4

6. Is the word *relationships* in paragraph 1 a compound word?

   Tick a box   YES ☐   NO ☐

   (Check Lit Tip 8)

7. What is a blood relation?

   A   a relative who is upsetting other family members

   B   the spouse of a husband's brothers

   C   anyone who knows their grandparents

   D   a person who is related to another by birth

8. According to the Eather family tree how many of the people shown are blood relations to David?

   A   3   B   5

   C   7   D   9

Need to try another chart? Check the contents page.

Lit Tip 10 – Improve your Literacy skills   **Showing and not telling**

A technique story tellers use is *show and **not** tell*. It's a good writing 'trick'.
It means story writers let readers use their own imaginations.
A simple example: You might write: 1. Bill stood by the water and felt cold.
OR you might write: 2. Bill stood by the water and shivered.
In example 2 the <u>reader</u> works out that Bill was probably cold. It's showing, **not** telling. It lets the reader get involved in the story. You don't have to tell the reader everything!
Read this sentence.
Mum looked into my bedroom and smiled. What is Mum feeling? _____
Can you think of a reason why Mum might have felt that way? (Use your imagination.)
(No answer required.)

Understanding Year 6 Comprehension
A. Horsfield © Five Senses Education © W. Marlin

The Ballyhooley Steam Train

The Ballyhooley steam train runs on a short track in Port Douglas (QLD), catering for tourists. The excursion begins at a platform by the marina.

As a passenger this is what you will experience.

On pulling out from the Mirage Marina Station you will see many yachts and pleasure vessels at berths in the marina before you pass the Yacht Club.

The train then enters an area of mangroves which, if the tide is high, can be under water. The track then passes through a remnant of rainforest. There is a very short platform at the Douglas Back Packers, the first stop.

The mangroves continue until you pass the Ballyhooley Depot on the left. Here volunteers carry out minor maintenance and put the trains to bed at the end of the day.

Shortly after leaving the Depot you arrive at the Sheraton Country Club station where there are tennis courts and a clubhouse. The next stop is the QT Resort platform. You then pass several other resorts before rounding the long bend to the terminus at St Crispins. At the terminus you will be requested to alight while the locomotive is uncoupled and turned around. This is a safety requirement. While the loco is re-coupling the carriages may be briefly jolted. Many visitors enjoy watching and filming the engine steaming away to the turntable where it is rotated (by 3 or 4 man-power!) in readiness for the return trip along the same track.

The turn-around takes about 10 minutes. While at St Crispins you may be fortunate enough to spot one or two crocodiles in the tidal lake near the station. Baby crocs are also seen here.

The round trip usually takes around 55 minutes, depending upon how many stops are made for dropping off and picking up passengers.

Adapted from: Ballyhooley flier and www.ballyhooley.com.au

Understanding Recounts

Circle a letter to answer questions 1 to 8.

1. How long does the return trip on the Ballyhooley train take?

   A   several minutes
   B   about ten minutes
   C   about half an hour
   D   almost an hour

2. The last stop the Ballyhooley train makes before beginning the return journey is at

   A   Sheraton Country Club
   B   St Crispins
   C   QT Resort
   D   Ballyhooley Depot

3. The passengers are most likely to see crocodiles

   A   at St Crispins
   B   in the mangrove waters
   C   near the Ballyhooley Depot
   D   at the Yacht Club

4. What is the correct order of station stops for the train after leaving the marina station?

   A   Yacht Club, Sheraton Country Club, QT Resort, St Crispins
   B   Douglas Back Packers, QT Resort, St Crispins, Ballyhooley Depot
   C   Douglas Back Packers, Sheraton Country Club, QT Resort, St Crispins
   D   Yacht Club, Douglas Back Packers, QT Resort, St Crispins

5. The writer says, *put the trains to bed*, in paragraph 2.
   These words *put the trains to bed* are an example of

   A   a simile
   B   an acronym
   C   a euphemism
   D   personification

6. At St Crispins the train

   A   is uncoupled from the carriages and returns to the depot
   B   returns to the marina by a different route
   C   is turned around on a railway turntable for the return trip
   D   pushes the carriages back to the marina from behind

7. The text is written in

   A   first person   B   second person   C   third person

8. What is the main safety concerns the passengers have to contend with?

   A   avoiding crocodiles
   B   high tides in the mangroves
   C   getting off at the wrong stop
   D   carriage jolting as the train recouples

Need to try another recount? Check the contents page.

Lit Tip 11 – Improve your literacy skills   **Person (or point of view)**

Did you have a problems with Q7? Here is some help.
Person in text refers to how the story is told or who the text is intended for.
There are three approaches to person in a text:
We use the terms first, second and third to refer to person.

Writing in **first person** uses personal pronouns of *I, we, me and us*. It may include *my, mine*, and *ours*.
The writer speaks about what he/she did. *I* is very common in first person writing.
Second person uses *you* as well as *your*. The writer speaks to the reader.
Third person uses pronouns such as *he, she, it, they* and *them*. Many books are written in third person.
Look back at Text 1 *Cat v Plant*. What person is it written in? _____

Understanding Year 6 Comprehension
A. Horsfield © Five Senses Education © W. Marlin

Rickshaw Rides in Vietnam

A ride in a bicycle rickshaw can be both frightening and fun at the same time. Sitting in a little cart being pulled or pushed by a man riding a bicycle through heavy traffic is not for the faint hearted.

In the city of Hanoi the traffic is constant. Motor scooters, cars, trucks, pedestrians and other rickshaws are all around you, ducking and weaving through the steady flow. While road rules seem non-existent, and as we were told with some humour "pedestrian crossings are just for decoration", everyone is very considerate and accidents are rare. A little bump causing a flat tyre is mended on the spot in a matter of seconds and before you know it you are off again, trying to catch up to the tour group ahead of you.

In the country the dirt roads are pot-holed and rutted and while your rickshaw bicycle rider is careful, the pot holes are hard to miss, the seats are narrow and hard, and the trip exhilarating but less than comfortable.

Rickshaw rides were a common form of transport a hundred years ago, but now they are mainly used for tourism throughout Asia.

A variation of the rickshaw is the auto rickshaw also known as the tuk-tuk or trishaw which is a motorised version and used as urban transport in many developing countries.

Travelling by tourist coach may be safe, but if you want to see a city from a different perspective, then a bicycle rickshaw ride is hard to beat. It can be noisy as horns are essential on cars, motor bikes and scooters, and are used constantly to signal—move over please, I'm coming through.

For anyone planning a trip to Vietnam a bicycle rickshaw is a must. And when you get to the end of your ride, there will be a man waiting to sell you a photo of your experience.

Elaine Horsfield

1. What does the writer see as an advantage of rickshaws over coaches?
    A   the rickshaw passenger can buy their photo after the ride
    B   drivers of rickshaws can manipulate the traffic better than coaches
    C   the noise of horns when travelling in coaches is constant
    D   rickshaw travellers get a better look at the surroundings

2. In paragraph 3 the writer says a rickshaw ride can be *exhilarating*.
   By saying it is *exhilarating* she means the experience is
    A   thrilling and fun   B   beneficial and rewarding
    C   overwhelming and scary   D   uncomfortable and dangerous

3. A modern version of the rickshaw experience is to have
    A   the passenger sit behind the driver   B   a ride on a coach
    C   the passenger on a seat at the front   D   a machine pull the rickshaw

4. According to the writer what can make a rickshaw ride unpleasant?
    A   the rudeness of other road users   B   the poor quality of the roads
    C   the possibility of flat tyres   D   large tourist coaches on the streets

5. What does the phrase, pedestrian crossings are just for decoration (paragraph 2),
   suggest about the traffic rules in a Vietnamese city?
    A   street markings are attractive   B   pedestrians are safe on crossings
    C   no one takes any notice of them   D   pedestrian crossings need painting

6. According to the text which statement is CORRECT?
    A   There are two seating positions for passengers on rickshaws.
    B   Coach travel through Vietnamese cities is not permitted.
    C   Travelling by rickshaw is a common form of transport for local people.
    D   The sounding of a horn is a sign that someone is being inconsiderate.

7. Which word best describes the rickshaw operators?
    A   thoughtless   B   efficient   C   lazy   D   harassed

8. It is most likely the writer wrote this text as a
    A   coach passenger   B   worker in Vietnam
    C   visitor to Vietnam   D   rickshaw driver

Lit Tip 12 – Improve your Literacy skills   Topic sentences

The **topic sentence** tells you what a paragraph is about. It is the most important sentence in a paragraph. It contains the main idea of a paragraph. The main idea will tell you what the rest of the sentences (details) in a paragraph are about.

The topic sentence in the first paragraph of the above text is: *A ride in a bicycle rickshaw can be both frightening and fun at the same time.* The rest is detail.
Underline the topic sentence in the next paragraph.
Find the topic sentence in the second paragraph in Exercise 2, *The Blob*.

Footprints in the Sand

(Eddie has spent a restless night sleeping in a beach hut on a remote tropical island. Now read on.)

I was up just as dawn broke. The early morning chorus of birds had just begun. The southern sky was a pink, pearly hue.

I decided on a short beach walk before getting breakfast. I went barefoot onto the tide-washed sand. It was still cool and damp.

It was a bit of a shock to discover another set of footprints. I looked up and down the beach, not sure what I was expecting to see. I tried peering into the early morning shadows of the beach vegetation. Nothing.

I felt a bit like Robinson Crusoe the day he found the footprints of Friday on his beach. I followed the prints along the beach. Every so often they would disappear where the wash of a larger wave had swept up onto the beach.

To my surprise, or maybe dismay, I suddenly came upon a second set of prints. There was not just one man but two men. Momentarily I questioned why I had assumed they were the prints of men. It was more to do with the size rather than any real evidence.

I stopped and sucked at my lips. Evidently the second person had been walking in the shallow water of the small waves as they ran up the beach.

Where are they now, I thought with growing alarm. What were they doing on the island anyway? Then my imagination kicked in like an angry mule. Why had I assumed that there were only two? There could have been a third person walking in the water. Or a fourth! Or a fifth!

Was there a whole a group of natives out there waiting for me to pass, then take over the hut? I thought about the hut's security. There was none!

I kept walking down the beach, away from the hut, following the footsteps but irrationally not treading on them in case I was destroying some sort of evidence.

I was near the end of the beach when I looked up at a little outcrop of ancient coral rock. Sitting in the meagre shade of a pandanus tree, half hidden by small coastal brush, were two men. Their bodies were dark against the early morning sky.

From: The Rats of Wolfe Island, A. Horsfield ebook available
https://authors-unlimited.org/book-member/the-rats-of-wolfe-island

Understanding Narratives   Circle a letter or write an answer for questions 1 to 8.

1. The most likely reason the narrator rose early for a walk was because he
    A   wanted to find out who had been walking along the beach
    B   needed to make preparations for breakfast
    C   woken by the noise of early morning bird calls
    D   enjoyed the tranquillity of the that time of the day

2. What was the first thing that made the narrator feel apprehensive?
    A   the chorus of the early morning birds
    B   the first set of footprints in the sand
    C   the lack of security at the beach hut
    D   the natives resting in the shade of a pandanus

3. What is the present tense of the word felt as used in the text?
    Write your answer on the line. _____

> If needed, check out
> Lit Tip 13 for help.

4. Why did the narrator assume the footsteps in the sand belonged to men?
    A   women were unlikely to be walking along the beach at that time
    B   men were the only other people staying in the beach hut
    C   there were two men sitting on a rock at the end of the beach
    D   the footprints were made by someone with large feet

5. What did the narrator assume about the owners of the footprints?
    A   They were lost.   B   They were about to attack.
    C   They were criminals.   D   They were hunting for food.

6. What can be assumed about the location of the narrator's beach hut?
    A   It was isolated.   B   It was subjected to break-ins.
    C   It was part of a large complex.   D   It was well appointed.

7. Before discovering the footprints the narrator was
    A   relaxed   B   moody   C   charming   D   bold

8. Which observation increased the narrator's concern for his safety?
    A   shadows in the beach vegetation   B   waves washing up the beach
    C   finding a second set of prints   D   the colour of the early morning sky

Lit Tip 13 – Improve your Literacy skills   Irregular verbs

To form the past tense of most verbs you add *ed*; e.g. yell – yelled
Some verbs change form. These verbs are called irregular verbs.
Examples: run/ran, write/wrote, see/saw. *Put* and *hit* do not change at all!
Give the past tense of these irregular verbs.

draw _____, have _____, keep _____, give _____

bite _____, tear _____, shake _____, ring _____

Understanding Year 6 Comprehension
A. Horsfield © Five Senses Education © W. Marlin

Lone Dog

I'm a lean dog, a mean dog, a wild dog, and lone;

I'm a rough dog, a tough dog, hunting on my own;

I'm a bad dog, a mad dog, teasing silly sheep;

I love to sit and <u>bay at the moon</u>, to keep fat souls from sleep.

I'll never be a lap dog, licking dirty feet,

A sleek dog, a meek dog, cringing for my meat,

Not for me the fireside, the well-filled ____(8)____,

But shut door, and sharp stone, and cuff and kick, and hate.

Not for me the other dogs, running by my side,

Some have run a short while, but none of them would bide.

O mine is still the lone trail, the hard trail, the best,

Wide wind, and wild stars, and hunger of the quest!

Irene McLeod (1885–1977)

Understanding Poetry

Circle a letter or write an answer for questions 1 to 8.

1. The lone dog wants to

    A   be fed meat   B   run with other dogs

    C   have freedom   D   sit on a person's lap

2. The lone dog loves to bay at the moon. This means the lone dog

    A   howls at the moon

    B   watches the moon rise over water

    C   sees the reflection of the moon in water

    D   is driven mad by the moon

3. The lone dog says not for me … *the sharp stone.*
What is the *sharp stone* he is most likely referring to?

    A   any stone he treads on

    B   a stone thrown to hurt him

    C   the stone from a type of fruit

    D   stones people use on their paths

4. What word in the third stanza means: remain or stay with someone or some animal
Write your answer on the line. _____

5. What does the lone dog do to show he is mean?

    A   He hunts on his own.   B   He cringes for his meat.

    C   He licks dirty feet.   D   He keeps fat people awake.

6. The lone dog would see his life as being one of

    A   satisfaction   B   misfortune   C   starvation   D   regret

7. The 'lone dog' could be best described as

    A   a yapping dog   B   an independent dog

    C   a pet dog   D   a working dog

8. A word has been deleted from the poem.
Which word would be best suited to the space (8)?

    A   bowl   B   stomach   C   crate   D   plate

Lit Tip 14 – Improve your literacy skills   Better words than *ate*

It is easy to overuse the *touch* type words in story writing. More precise words are available which can improve your story.
Look at these three examples:
1. Fay touched the pillow.   2. Fay patted the pillow.   3. Fay poked the pillow.

Examples 2 and 3 give the reader different insights into Fay's feelings.
Here are some other options: caressed, stroked, gripped, prodded, thumped

Find four better words than ate that help readers get a more precise picture of Kelly.
Kelly ate the pie.

1. _____   2. _____   3. _____   4. _____

Understanding Year 6 Comprehension
A. Horsfield © Five Senses Education © W. Marlin

Traffic Gridlock: A Global Problem

Traffic in Hanoi, Vietnam
Photo: A Horsfield

There are at least 8 lines of traffic waiting for the lights to change.

There are more and more people and more and more vehicles on our roads—not only in Vietnam but also in all Australian cities.

Traffic is a big problem in many cities around the world. Traffic is especially bad during rush hour—morning and afternoon—the times when people go to work or school and the time when they go home. Many people take buses, subways, trains or ferries to work, but many other people drive their private vehicles. As a result, many streets and arterial roads are very busy and traffic is very heavy, often choked with frustrated drivers. Often the traffic does not move—this is called gridlock. Streets and roads are huge parking lots!

Many cities are trying to solve their traffic problems. Some cities are building more roads. Other cities are expanding their public transport systems—buses, ferries and subways.

Many cities are trying to reduce the number of cars on their roads. Some major roads have carpool lanes—special lanes for cars with two, three or more people. In some cities, people drive their cars only on certain days of the week. For example, in Athens, people with licence plate numbers ending in 0 to 4 drive on some days and people with numbers ending in 5 to 9 drive on other days.

Australian cities often have designated bus lanes—lanes restricted to buses. Buses can carry more people more quickly to city centres with special bus lanes. Bus lanes are better for moving people than cars with just one driver and no passengers.

Every day, around the world, more and more people drive to and from work in more and more cars. As a result, traffic is a global problem.

Adapted from: an idea in Side by Side (3rd Ed) S. J Molinski and B Bliss Lonmans 2001

Understanding Opinions

Circle a letter to answer questions 1 to 8.

1. What does *gridlock* actually refer to?
   - A   a situation of severe traffic congestion
   - B   a framework of fixed rows and columns
   - C   cars unable to move across an intersection
   - D   traffic moving slowly along a major road artery

2. The writer uses the words: more and more people and more and more vehicles
   The use of *more* four times in a short piece of text is
   - A   an example the writer's limited vocabulary
   - B   to emphasise the severity of the problem
   - C   a failure to understand the severity of the problem
   - D   to poke fun at a complex and serious issue

3. According to the text many people avoid driving in rush hour traffic by
   - A   by-passing major roads
   - B   buying a motor cycle
   - C   using special number plates
   - D   riding on public transport

4. What is the most likely reason the writer produced this text?
   - A   to compare traffic in different cities
   - B   to recount a personal experience
   - C   to provoke awareness of a problem
   - D   to complain about traffic in Vietnam

5. As used in the text *arterial* roads are ones that are
   - A   congested
   - B   major urban routes
   - C   flowing with traffic
   - D   requiring upgrades

6. Which option is an example of a metaphor taken from the text?
   - A   at least 8 lines of traffic waiting
   - B   bus lanes are better for moving people
   - C   streets and roads are huge parking lots
   - D   traffic is a global problem

7. What would be a suitable synonym for *global*?
   - A   worldwide   B   national   C   immense   D   incredible

8. Some Australian city councils are trying to reduce traffic congestion by
   - A   encouraging people to ride motorbikes
   - B   restricting road use to specific cars on certain days
   - C   constructing more roads
   - D   dedicating some road lanes for bus use only

Lit Tip 15 – Improve your Literacy skills   **Words with many meanings**

If I said *watch* it could mean a timepiece, a looking action or a period of guard duty.
What a word means depends upon its context.
What word means:

1. charge with an offence: printed pages bound together _____

2. pellets of frozen rain: call out for a cab _____

3. a fruit: a shade of yellow: a badly made car _____

Understanding Year 6 Comprehension
A. Horsfield © Five Senses Education © W. Marlin

The Forbidden Billabong

For years the young man had warned his two young brothers not to fish in the nearby billabong. And while they had respected his advice there had never been a problem.

As the boys grew older they began to question his warning. What could possibly be wrong with the billabong? It was deep and dark, certainly. But why should they not fish there?

"Because I say so," the older brother repeated.

It was a silly reply, because the boys needed an explanation that would make sense of the warning.

"With so many fish confined in the billabong, they should be easy to catch. Why ignore a source of food?" the boys asked in frustration.

"The answer is very simple," explained the older brother at last. "The Elders warned me when I was a child that water spirits protected the billabong, and I always heed the Elders' warnings. I have never fished in that billabong and neither can you two. And that is the end of the matter," he added impatiently as he walked away.

The two boys waited until the older brother was out of sight then, exchanging mischievous grins, they bolted off to collect their fishing spears.

The billabong became strangely quiet as the boys approached. Birds stopped singing. The low murmur of insects hushed. The breeze became so still that not a leaf rustled.

The boys were much too excited to notice. They could hardly believe how crowded the billabong was with big fish. When they raised their spears to catch them, however, the spears slipped from their grasp. Their hands had changed into webbed claws!

The boys had discovered in the worst possible way that their older brother had told them the truth. The water spirits that protected the billabong had changed them into platypuses. And they were forced to enter the inky depths to join all the others who had ignored the Elders' warnings in the past.

Adapted from: Even more tales of my Grandmother's Dreamtime by Naiura, Bartel Publications 2010.

Understanding Legends

Circle a letter to answer questions 1 to 8.

1. The two young brothers believed that
   - A the young man had invented the story about the water spirits
   - B the fish in the billabong were not worth catching
   - C warnings about the billabong were real
   - D the Elders' advice didn't apply to them

2. What reason did the young man give for advising his brothers **not** to fish in the billabong?
   - A the billabong was deep and dark
   - B insects infested the billabong
   - C water spirits protected the billabong
   - D platypuses lived in the billabong

3. A legend is a form of
   - A narrative
   - B report
   - C explanation
   - D persuasive text

4. What was the relationship between the young man and the two brothers?
   - A He was a friendly old fisherman.
   - B He was an older brother.
   - C He was an elder of the tribe.
   - D He was one of the water spirits.

5. What was the first thing the younger brothers saw at the billabong?
   - A large fish
   - B water spirits
   - C murmuring insects
   - D platypuses

6. According to the text which statement is CORRECT?
   - A Fishermen went to the billabong to catch platypuses.
   - B The young man ignored the warning not to fish in the billabong.
   - C The two brothers took the young man's warning seriously.
   - D The brothers were not the first people to ignore the warning.

7. Which word from the text is a compound word?
   - A platypuses
   - B billabong
   - C nearby
   - D discovered

8. A suitable alternate title for the text would be
   - A Fishing
   - B The price of disobedience
   - C By the billabong
   - D Two young brothers

Lit Tip 16 – Improve your Literacy skills   Sentence beginnings – And

Did you notice that the last sentence began with *And*. *You* may have been told **not** to start sentences with *And*. Most of the time this is good advice.

And can be used as a literary device. It may be used to emphasise a point.

Use *And* if you have a reason but don't use it too much. Remember the traditional tale, *The Little Red Hen*? The final sentence is: *And* she did!

It is not good writing to use it repeatedly as a conjunction to join sentences or ideas.

Check out the last sentence of Passage 12 *Rickshaw Rides*.

The writer has used an *And* sentence to round off her report.

Understanding Year 6 Comprehension
A. Horsfield © Five Senses Education © W. Marlin

One Classy Car – The Duesenberg Story

Duesenberg Automobile & Motors Company (sometimes referred to as "Duesy") was an American manufacturer of luxury cars. Founded by brothers August and Frederick Duesenberg it operated from 1913 to 1937.

The Duesenberg story is a story of two immigrant brothers and a dream to build the world's finest car. They migrated to the US in 1884 with their widowed mother and four other children where they were raised on a farm.

A few years after leaving school the pair teamed up to open a bicycle shop but they quickly moved into the automobile business. They built their first automobile in 1906. In 1913 they established the Duesenberg Automobile & Motors Company specialising in racing cars and powerboat engines.

The brothers were self-taught engineers and built many experimental cars. Duesenberg cars were considered the top cars of the time, and were built entirely by hand. The Duesenberg name was noticed when in 1914, Eddie Rickenbacker, a World War I fighter pilot ace, drove a "Duesy" to finish in 10th place at the famous Indianapolis 500 car race. In 1921 the first American to win the French Grand Prix drove a Duesenberg to victory. Duesenberg won the Indianapolis 500 car race in 1924, 1925, and 1927.

As the company evolved Frederick was given 'free reign' to produce "the greatest automobile ever produced in America". He produced his Model J car within two years. It was a 265 horsepower car.

Only the rich and powerful owned Duesenbergs, including film stars, European royalty—and Al Capone, the gangster. The cars combined luxury, style and elegance with the mechanical precision and amazing acceleration and astounding speed. Almost 500 cars were produced.

Frederick died in 1932 while road testing a customer's car. August continued to be involved in the manufacturing of the Duesenberg until the company closed its doors in 1937. The car is now a valuable collectors' item.

Because of the Deusenberg's amazing <u>attributes</u>, the phrase "it's a doozy" re-emerged in the 1930s to describe something that had the best of everything.

Sources: http://classiccars.about.com/od/classiccarsaz/a/Duesenberg.htm
Notice board display in Warbirds and Wheels Museum, Wanaka NZ
http://en.wikipedia.org/wiki/Duesenberg

Understanding Recounts

Circle a letter or write an answer for questions 1 to 8.

1. In which year did the Duesenberg brothers build their first car?

   A 1906   B 1913   C 1914   D 1932

2. What was the fate of Frederick Duesenberg?

   A He left the car company to build bicycles.

   B He went to France to compete in car races.

   C He died in a car crash while road testing a Duesenberg.

   D He closed the company that manufactured Duesenbergs.

3. Which word best describes the Duesenberg cars?

   A prestigious   B overrated   C ostentatious   D ordinary

4. Write the numbers 1 to 4 in the boxes to show the correct order in which events occurred in the recount. The first one (1) has been done for you.

	the first American to win the French Grand Prix drove a Duesenberg
1	the Duesenberg brothers open a bicycle shop in the United States
	the Duesenberg brothers build their first car
	the Duesenberg company ceases to make automobiles

5. Which fact implies that the Duesenberg brothers were highly respected car builders?

   A Their company lasted from 1913 until 1937.

   B Duesenberg cars won the Indianapolis 500 car races in the 1920s.

   C The Model J Duesenberg was a 265 horsepower car.

   D The Duesenberg car became a collectors' item.

6. The Duesenberg cars were designed to appeal to

   A families   B the rich and famous

   C the average citizen   D car collectors

7. In the text the Duesenberg is described as having amazing *attributes*.
   A suitable synonym to replace *attributes* in the text would be

   A details   B accessories   C qualities   D attractions

8. If something is described as a 'doozy' it implies it

   A is suitable for top competitions   B uses showy elegance to impress

   C is without an equal   D has been made to a high standard

---

Lit Tip 17 – Improve your Literacy skills   **Comparative adjectives**

With most short words the comparative adjectives follow this pattern.

Examples: Start with *fast* and it's *fast<u>er</u>* and *fast<u>est</u>*, or *happy, happi<u>er</u>, happi<u>est</u>*
'Longer' words tend to use a different form: *graceful, <u>more</u> graceful, <u>most</u> graceful.*
There are a few common exceptions: *good, better, best* (not *gooder* or *goodest* !);
bad, worse, worst; little, less, least and *far, further, furthest.*
Clever is *more* clever and *most* clever and *bitter* is <u>more</u> bitter and <u>most</u> bitter.

Complete these patterns.
old, _____, _____, some, more, _____
Some adjectives do not have degrees of comparison, e.g. *dead, unique* and *perfect.*

Understanding Year 6 Comprehension
A. Horsfield © Five Senses Education © W. Marlin

Interjections

Definition:

1. a word or words, or some noises, used to express surprise, dismay, pain or feelings and emotions: Ouch! That hurts!

2. to say something which interrupts what one, or someone else, is saying.

Interjections are often short exclamations like Oh!, Hmm! or Ah! They have no real grammatical value but we use them a lot, more in speaking than in writing. An interjection is sometimes followed by an exclamation mark (!) when written.

Interjections, such as *er* and *um*, are called hesitation devices—very common in English. They are used when the speaker is unsure what to say.

It's important to know what interjections mean when people use them. This list shows some interjections with examples.

Interjection	Meaning	Example
ah	expressing pleasure	Ah! that feels good.
ah	expressing understanding	Ah! Now I get it.
oh dear	expressing pity	Of dear! What a shame.
eh	asking for repetition	"It's hot tonight." 'Eh!"
hi	expressing a greeting	Hi! How are you?
hey	calling for attention	Hey! Come here.
oh	expressing surprise	Oh! How did it happen?
ouch	expressing pain	Ouch! That hurt.
well	expressing surprise	Well! I never!

There may be more than 150 common interjections.

These words are often used as interjections: bon voyage, bother, boy, bravo, come on, goodness, hello, indeed, know, like, man, mean, my, no sweat, peace, rather, right on, rot, so,

Carefully used interjections can improve the writing of your narratives. Here are a few you could use.

Absolutely	Amen	Boo	Ha	Rats
Achoo	Anytime	Bravo	Hey	Uggh
Ahh	Argh	Cheers	Hi	Waa
Aha	Anyhow	Drat	Hmm	What
Ahem	As if	Eek	Huh	Whoa
Ahoy	Aww	Eh	Indeed	Woops
Agreed	Bah	Gee	Oops	Wow
Alas	Behold	Golly	Ouch	Yay
Alright	Bingo	Goodness	Phew	Yes
Alrighty	Bless you	Gosh	Please	Yikes

Understanding Explanations

Circle a letter or write an answer for questions 1 to 8.

1. An interjection is often used

    A   to offend people

    B   to interrupt someone who is speaking

    C   after much careful consideration

    D   when making a phone order

2. A real word can also be used as an interjection.
   Is this TRUE or FALSE? Tick a box.   TRUE ☐   FALSE ☐

3. The interjection, *Whoa* is used to tell someone to

    A   stop doing something   B   be careful

    C   look at something   D   get out of the way

4. What noise could you make to show disapproval?

    A   a sucking noise   B   a sigh of relief

    C   a whistle   D   a tongue clicking sound

5. What feeling is a speaker expressing when they say, *Oh dear*?

    A   hope   B   amusement

    C   pity   D   understanding

6. Interjections are most often used in

    A   everyday conversations

    B   speech writing

    C   newspaper articles

    D   driving instructions

7. Which interjection would most likely be used if someone were suddenly successful?

    A   Ooh   B   Bingo   C   Eek   D   Ahh

8. You are writing a story. A character wants to attract someone's attention.
   Which would be the most suitable interjection for that character to use?

    A   Boo   B   Well   C   Darn   D   Ahoy

Lit Tip 18 – Improve your Literacy skills   **Interjections**

You have just read about **interjections**.
Interjections in narrative conversations can show things about the characters.

What interjection could you use to show:

a pleasant surprise _____   a sudden pain _____

unsure about an idea _____   the sight of blood _____

Choose a suitable interjection to complete this sentence? (Circle a letter.)

" _____, you can't do that!' yelled the ranger.

A Hey   B Err   C So   D Yeah   E Yippee

Interjections are a exriting device, but don't use them too often.

Understanding Year 6 Comprehension
A. Horsfield © Five Senses Education © W. Marlin

Poochera Ants

Poochera is a small South Australian town. It has an obscure claim to fame. Poochera is home to the prehistoric ant named *Nothomyrmecia macrops*. Amongst entomologists this ant is considered a living fossil, the world's most primitive living ant.

Nothomyrmecia was discovered in 1931 near Balladonia in Western Australia. Its discovery caused a great deal of excitement. The species was seen as living proof that ants had evolved from wasps. Embarrassingly however, further specimens were unobtainable as amateur naturalists from a 1931 expedition failed to find any of the ants.

The year 1977 saw Nothomyrmecia fortuitously rediscovered by Dr Bob Taylor and a party of entomologists from Canberra. The story is a ____(7)____ one.

Spurred on by rumours that an American scientist was coming to search for the lost ant, Dr Taylor apparently mounted one last ditch attempt to beat the Americans to the punch. By an incredible stroke of good luck Dr Taylor and his team were driving to Western Australia when their vehicle struck mechanical problems at Poochera. The expedition was forced to camp there for the night.

That evening Dr Taylor conducted an impromptu insect survey in the mallee scrub adjacent to camp. There's no doubt the last thing on Dr Taylor's mind was Nothomyrmecia.

After all, the last and only recorded sighting was made 46 years earlier, and even that was 1300 kilometres to the west. Poochera was definitely the last place where Dr Taylor expected to find Nothomyrmecia—but there it was, one solitary worker ant crawling on a eucalyptus tree trunk.

The sight was truly astonishing. Dr Taylor then rushed back to his colleagues and in true Australian style he announced to the world, "The bloody ant's here! I've got the Notho-bloody-myrmecia!"

Today the Poochera is a favoured site for ant entomologists during winter and spring, when Nothomyrmecia is at its most active. Nothomyrmecia is considered a very rare ant, and is rated as critically endangered. Since the Poochera rediscovery one further Nothomyrmecia colony has been found at Penong, 180 kilometres to the west. However, the fate of the original Western Australian population remains a mystery.

Adapted from: http://www.nullarbornet.com.au/towns/poochera.html

Understanding Recounts

Circle a letter or write an answer for questions 1 to 8.

1. Where is the town of Poochera?
   - A   in remote South Australia
   - B   near Balladonia in Western Australia
   - C   in an American state
   - D   around Canberra

2. What motivated Dr Taylor to make a decision to look for *Nothomyrmecia macrops*?
   - A   the likelihood the ant may become extinct
   - B   the threat of an American team finding the ant
   - C   an opportunity to visit Poochera
   - D   a report that the ants had been seen in Penong

3. An entomologist is a person who
   - A   has an interest in camping
   - B   travels in remote areas
   - C   explores the outback
   - D   studies insects

4. The saying *beat someone to the punch* means
   - A   acting with unnecessary aggression
   - B   being first to get a refreshing drink
   - C   act before someone else to gain an advantage
   - D   to down a boxing opponent

5. Why had Nothomyrmecia found near Belladonia in 1931 created scientific interest?
   - A   it had migrated from Western Australian to South Australia
   - B   it was believed to be the world's most primitive ant
   - C   it could not be found by amateur naturalists in the same year
   - D   it appeared to have disappeared after the first discovery

6. The discovery of Nothomyrmeciama near Poochera could be best described as
   - A   a lucky break
   - B   the reward for detailed research
   - C   a clumsy miscalculation
   - D   the result of painstaking exploration

7. A word has been deleted from the text.
   Which word would be best suited to the space (7)?
   - A   improbable
   - B   fanciful
   - C   remarkable
   - D   staggering

8. What part of speech is *living* as used in paragraph 1?
   - A   verb
   - B   adjective
   - C   adverb
   - D   noun

Lit Tip 19 – Improve your Literacy skills   **Swearing in text**

Adding expletives (swear words, blasphemy) is not encouraged in primary school writing or in official correspondence. Expletives usually do not improve the writing.

There can be some exceptions, such as *bloody* in the above recount. It signifies a critical moment for a character.

Swearing is common. There is a way around adding swearing to text without being explicit. Use indirect speech (reported speech). The text from the above passage could be written in indirect speech as: *Dr Taylor swore excitedly when he discovered the ant*. This way the reader can use his/her imagination and the writer does not offend the reader. It is a clever writing technique.

Understanding Year 6 Comprehension
A. Horsfield © Five Senses Education © W. Marlin

Read this narrative extract from *Treasure Island.*

Treasure Island

(Chapter 32 The voice among the trees)

(The pirates are resting before continuing their way to find the treasure. They have taken young Jim Hawkins as prisoner. He relates the story. Now read on.)

Ever since they had found the skeleton they had spoken lower and lower, and they had almost got to whispering by now, so that the sound of their talk hardly interrupted the silence of the woods. All of a sudden, out of the middle of the trees in front of us, a thin, high, trembling voice struck up the well known words: "Fifteen men on the dead man's chest — Yo-ho-ho, and a bottle of rum!"

I never have seen men more dreadfully affected than the pirates. The colour went from their six faces like enchantment. Some leaped to their feet, some clawed hold of others and Morgan grovelled on the ground.

"It's Flint, by ----!" cried Isaac Merry.

The song had stopped as suddenly as it began, as though someone had laid his hand upon the singer's mouth. Coming through the clear, sunny atmosphere among the green treetops, I thought it had sounded airily and sweetly but the effect on my companions was the stranger.

"Come," said Long John Silver, struggling with his ashen lips to get the word out; "this won't do. Stand by to go about. This is a rum start, and I can't name the voice, but it's someone skylarking-someone that's flesh and blood, and you may bet on that."

His courage had come back as he spoke, and some of the colour to his face along with it. Already the others had begun to lend an ear to this encouragement and were coming a little to themselves, when the same voice broke out again-not this time singing, but in a faint distant hail that echoed yet fainter among the cliffs of Spyglass Hill.

"Darby M'Graw," it wailed—for that is the word that best describes the sound—"Darby M'Graw! Darby M'Graw!" again and again and again—and then rising a little higher, and with an oath that I leave out, "Fetch aft the rum, Darby!"

The buccaneers remained rooted to the ground, their eyes starting from their heads. Long after the voice had died away they still stared in silence, dreadfully, before them.

"That fixes it!" gasped Merry. "Let's go."

"They was his last words," moaned Morgan. "His last words above board."

Adapted from: Treasure Island by Robert Louis Stevenson (1850 - 1894).

Understanding Narratives

Circle a letter or write an answer for questions 1 to 8.

1. What had terrified the pirates?
   - A the finding of a skeleton
   - B the singing of someone believed dead
   - C the words of Long John Silver
   - D the silence following the singing

2. How did the pirates react to an earlier discovery of a skeleton?
   - A they became subdued
   - B they were unconcerned
   - C they argued amongst themselves
   - D they hurried to Spyglass Hill

3. From the text which word has Stevenson used as a synonym for pirates?
   Write your answer on the line. _____

4. How did Morgan react to the sound coming from the trees?
   - A his lips went white
   - B he clutched onto other pirates
   - C he leaped about wildly
   - D he crawled about on the ground

5. The pirates began to *lend an ear* to Silver's reasoning.
   What does the term *lend an ear* mean?
   - A turn one's head to have an ear facing the speaker
   - B cap one's ear with the hand to improve hearing
   - C to listen carefully especially to someone with advice
   - D getting prepared to argue a decision

6. Who was the least upset by the sound of singing?
   - A Long John Silver
   - B Isaac Merry
   - C the narrator (Jim Hawkins)
   - D Darby M'Graw

7. The text is written in   (For help, check out Lit **Tip 11**)
   - A first person
   - B second person
   - C third person

8. When Merry heard the name Darby M'Graw called out he wanted
   - A to find out who the caller was
   - B to get far away from the location
   - C Silver to take some action
   - D to continue searching for the treasure

Lit Tip 20 – Improve your literacy skills **Alliteration**

Alliteration is the use of the same letter or sound at the beginning of words that are close
together in the text, especially poetry: green grass, cocky cooks
Alliteration can be used to add interest to your prose writing.
Underline the letters that are used for alliteration in these examples.
1. French fries   **2.** strong and sturdy   **3.** raging, ranting rabble
Add a noun to these adjectives to make examples of alliteration (e.g. black blot).

1. _____ shirt,   2. _____ street,

3. _____ test,   4. _____ cowboy

Often alliteration is used effectively for words that resemble sounds (**onomatopoeia**): thud and thump,
whistling wind, clip clop.

Understanding Year 6 Comprehension
A. Horsfield © Five Senses Education © W. Marlin

Film review
Race to Witch Mountain

Duration: 100 mins
Rated: PG

Race to Witch Mountain is a 2009 science fiction / thriller film and is a continuation of the 1975 Disney film Escape to Witch Mountain. Three versions of the film have been produced: 1975, 1995 and 2009.

Your parents probably loved this film – 40 years ago when they were kids! Whenever an old favourite movie is remade you hope that it will bring something new to the film but if you're expecting to see anything of the 70s classic Escape to Witch Mountain in this 'remake', then think again – while Race to Witch Mountain has taken some of the story line of the original, it has re-imagined it in a whole new way.

When a UFO falls to earth in the Nevada desert, taxi driver Jack Bruno thinks nothing of it—until he finds himself with two unlikely customers in the back seat of his cab. Are they helpless children or the most unlikely aliens we'll ever see? After being chased all over Las Vegas (and through a hilarious UFO convention), Jack has no choice but to help the kids' get back to their spaceship.

Race to Witch Mountain is stuffed full of big budget effects—there are loads of car chases, bad guys (both alien and government officials) and some pretty impressive alien stunts too. While there is a little violence in the movie, Race to Witch Mountain is sure to be a hit with the whole family.

The films were based on the 1968 novel, Escape to Witch Mountain by Alexander Key.

This text was adapted from a review written by Ella Walsh for Kidspot—Australia's parenting resource for family entertainment.

Rating ★ ★ ★ ★ ☆

Sources: http://en.wikipedia.org/wiki/Science_fiction_film
Adapted from: http://www.kidspot.com.au/Preschool-Behaviour-Race-to-Witch-Mountain+2145+33+article.htm
Permission applied for on 17/6/14
(Kidspot.com.au, Level 5, HWT Tower 40 City Road, Southbank VIC, Australia 3006)

Understanding Film Reviews

Circle a letter or write an answer for questions 1 to 8.

1. How many times has Escape to Witch Mountain been made into a film?

   Write your answer in the box. ☐

2. How might young viewers react to this film?
   They will most likely be

   | A | confused | B | excited | C | relaxed | D | upset |

3. What conclusion did the reviewer have of the film, Escape to Witch Mountain?
   - A the 2009 version was not as good as earlier versions of the film
   - B the film contained violence that could upset young children
   - C some humour in the film would have made it more enjoyable
   - D the film is suitable entertainment for the whole family

4. The film has big budget effects. What is implied by big budget effects?
   - A costly lighting, action and scenery
   - B an adventure film shot in remote locations
   - C an action movie where main costs are the violence scenes
   - D a production that spends more on visual effects than actors

5. The film is rated PG. This means it
   - A is for private viewing only
   - B has payment granted options
   - C is suitable for children if accompanied by an adult
   - D has potentially gruesome violence

6. The aliens in the film are most likely

   | A | children | B | monsters | C | taxi drivers | D | witches |

7. Who wrote the original story behind Escape to Witch Mountain?

   | A | Walt Disney | B | Alexander Key | C | Ella Walsh | D | Jack Bruno |

8. What does Jack Bruno end up doing?
   - A looking for the children's parents
   - B capturing a flying saucer
   - C taking the children to Las Vegas
   - D being abduced by aliens

Lit Tip 21 – Improve your literacy skills　　　**Initials or Acronyms**

Many institutions are referred to by initials or by acronyms.
What is the difference? **Initials** don't make words. For example, for Western Australia we say W then A. We don't say WA (to rhyme with ha).
Acronyms are words made from initials, e.g. for ANZAC we use capital letter and say the word not the separate letters. A few common nouns are formed from acronyms: radar, laser and scuba. Check out the meaning of radar.

Find 2 examples from the text of initials representing words. _____, _____

What does LCD stand for? _____
Tick the box if the initials form an acronym.

RAAF ☐　　PG ☐　　JP ☐　　OMG ☐　　WW1 ☐　　SOS ☐

43

Understanding Year 6 Comprehension
A. Horsfield © Five Senses Education © W. Marlin

Storm Surges

Tropical cyclones in Australia contain a range of dangerous hazards that include local rises in sea levels known as a storm surge or storm tide. When a storm surge arrives on top of a high tide, the resulting inundation can reach coastal areas that might otherwise have been safe.

Everyone living in a potential storm surge area should have a household emergency plan which includes evacuation and shelter considerations. Preparations need to be in place to shelter in a secure place either at home or with family and friends.

The best option for most people during a cyclone is to shelter in their own homes. This questionnaire/chart can help work out if there is a need to make evacuation plans.

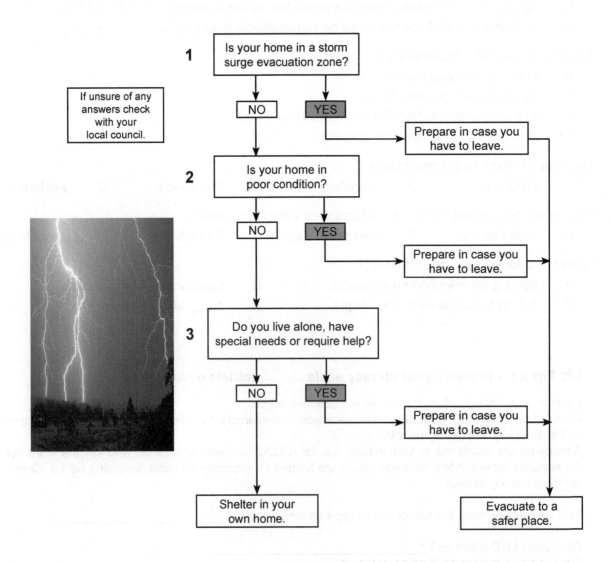

Adapted from: StormTide Cyclone Shelter - Cairns Regional Council.

Understanding Flow Charts

Circle a letter or write an answer for questions 1 to 8.

1. What two conditions contribute to a storm surge?
   Write your answer in the spaces. 1 _____, 2 _____

2. The flow chart is intended to
   - A   help people make the right decision
   - B   warn people of the dangers of storm surges
   - C   encourage people to build stronger homes
   - D   dispel people's fears of storm surges

3. In which person is the text *Storm Surges* written? (Check out **Lit Tip 11**.)
   - A   first person
   - B   second person
   - C   third person

4. If a person's home is in a storm surge location and not in good condition they should
   - A   buy a new home in a safer area
   - B   ring their local council for help
   - C   have an emergency evacuation plan
   - D   be prepared to shelter in their own home

5. The **storm surge** flow chart is most like
   - A   a procedure
   - B   an explanation
   - C   a report
   - D   a recount

6. During a storm surge older people should remain in their homes if
   - A   they live alone
   - B   their home is in a storm surge evacuation zone
   - C   the council does not have an evacuation plan
   - D   they have a sturdy home

7. Which word from the text has a similar meaning to *inundation*?
   - A   surge
   - B   flooding
   - C   evacuation
   - D   hazards

8. If a person answers NO to all three questions they should
   - A   make immediate plans to leave
   - B   take refuge with a neighbour
   - C   evacuate to a secure site
   - D   remain in their homes

Lit Tip 22 – Improve your literacy skills   **Prefixes: micro and macro**

Micro is a prefix meaning very small. If something is microscopic it is too small to be seen by the naked eye. You may need a microscope.
A microwave oven is one that heats using very short electromagnetic waves.
A microchip is a very small unit placed under the skin of animals for identification.

What is a microbe? _____

The opposite of *micro* is *macro*. It is much less common in everyday usage and implies something is large or important. If something is macroscopic it is large enough to be seen by the naked eye.

A macropod is an animal with big feet. Name an Australian macropod. _____

Understanding Year 6 Comprehension
A. Horsfield © Five Senses Education © W. Marlin

Fjords and Sounds

A fjord (also spelled fiord) is a long, narrow ocean inlet with steep sides or cliffs. The word comes from Iceland. The coast of Norway, Iceland and Greenland's island have many fjords but there are fjords closer to Australia — in New Zealand, where they are called sounds. Milford Sound is the most famous.

A fjord is formed when a glacier cuts a U-shaped valley. The slow moving ice carves or gouges a path through the underlying bedrock below sea level. Most fjords were formed millions of years ago, during ice ages when the ocean level was lower.

Fjords generally have a shelf of bedrock at their mouth caused by the glacier's slower erosion rate. In many cases this still causes extreme currents and large saltwater rapids. Norway is recognised as having the world's strongest tidal current in and out of some of its fjords.

Milford Sound was formed when the sea entered a deeply excavated glacial trough after the ice melted. The thickness of the ice that excavated the basin can be gauged in the height of the vertical cliffs that rise from below sea level, revealing older U-shaped glacial 'hanging' valleys. These valleys are a feature of Milford Sound. Where once smaller glaciers served as tributaries to the main ice flow, streams now run and enter the principal valley as waterfalls.

The Bowen Falls has a sheer drop of 160m from a hanging valley into the sound. The Stirling Falls, with its permanent water flow, cascades into the sound like a giant shower with a drop of 146m. It is spectacular after rain. Mitre Peak (1692m) is the tallest mountain in the area rising straight from the sound. Its name comes from its twin peaks resembling a bishop's mitre (headdress).

Seal Point, at the mouth of the fjord, is one of the few areas in the fjord where seals can climb out of the water onto the rocks. While the seals settle there all year round, dolphins and penguins are regular inhabitants of the sound, while dolphins swim beside boats. Occasionally a whale makes its way into the sound.

Sources: http://www.milford-sound.nz.com/geography-wildlife.aspx
http://en.wikipedia.org/wiki/Fjord#Formation

Understanding Reports

Circle a letter or write an answer for questions 1 to 8.

1. What is another name for a fjord (or fiord)?
   Write your answer on the line. _____

2. The writer regards Milford Sound as

   A featureless   B impressive   C dangerous   D humdrum

3. Where are the 'hanging' valleys located?
   A high above the water of Milford Sound
   B at the mouth of Milford Sound
   C on the top of Mitre Peak
   D on a path through the underlying bedrock

4. What is the most likely reason seals may have difficulty climbing out of the waters of Milford Sound?
   A the coldness of the water   B the proximity of whales
   C the sheer cliff faces of the sound   D waterfalls gushing into the sound

5. Which words from the text is an example of a simile?
   A ice carves or gouges a path through the underlying bedrock
   B dolphins and penguins are regular inhabitants of the sound
   C fjords were formed millions of years ago
   D cascades into the sound like a giant shower

6. Where do the cliffs of Milford Sound begin?
   A at water level   B on the rock shelf
   C below sea level   D under the waterfalls

7. What word from the text has a similar meaning to *excavated*?
   A gouged   B entered   C formed   D gauged

8. What can make entering the mouth of a fjord hazardous?
   A the thickness of the ice   B saltwater rapids
   C waterfall pouring into the water   D an occasional whale

---

Lit Tip 23 – Improve your Literacy skills   **Pesky prepositions 1**

Prepositions are words that tell you the position of one thing in relation to another.
The word pre<u>position</u> contains the word <u>position</u>!
Some common prepositions are: in, by, beside, near, on, under, at, during, along
Use *between* when two things are involved - *between* the (2) goalposts.
Use *among* when many things are involved - *among* the (many people) crowd.
Of and *off* sound similar but have different meanings.
Compare: The box fell *off* the truck AND The sleeve *of* my coat is muddy.
Underline the correct preposition to complete these sentences.

1. Meg stood (between, among) her parents.   **2.** Lee sat in the back (of, off) the car.

3. A fork fell (of, off) the table.   **4.** Small birds hid (between, among) the leaves.

Understanding Year 6 Comprehension
A. Horsfield © Five Senses Education © W. Marlin

The Dogman

The dogman dangles from the clouds,

<u>Astride</u> a beam of swinging air

Unrealised hero of the crowds

Whose upturned faces dimly stare.

Like daisies from the ground

<u>Arrayed in far-off random files</u>

Their homage rises without a sound

In grave content or drifting smiles.

*Gulliver was a sailor washed ashore on Lilliput Island.
He awoke to find he couldn't move. He had hundreds
of tiny beings swarming all over his body.

The earth is open to his eyes

Spread before him like a chart

To the blue-washed blind of sea and sky

To where the mountains lie apart.

Beneath his feet the city falls

In patterns of great blocks and spires

A sumptuous Gulliver* who sprawls

In bond to man's minute desires.

Robert Clark 1911–2004

Understanding Poetry

Circle a letter or write an answer for questions 1 to 8.

1. Look at the photograph on the right. Which line or lines from the poem could it best illustrate?

    A The dogman dangles from the clouds, / Astride a beam of swinging air

    B Whose upturned faces dimly stare / Like daisies from the ground

    C Beneath his feet the city falls / In patterns of great blocks and spires

    D Unrealised hero of the crowds

2. The dogman could best be described as a

    A construction worker
    B dog pound operator
    C member of a rescue team
    D guide to city landmarks

3. Which word best describes the feeling of those watching the dogman?

    A amused
    B mesmerised
    C apprehensive
    D impressed

4. Which line from the poem is an example of a simile?

    A Spread before him like a chart

    B Whose upturned faces dimly stare

    C In grave content or drifting smiles

    D To the blue-washed blind of sea and sky

5. The word *astride* as used in stanza 1 means

    A walking boldly along a beam

    B legs apart while balanced on a steel beam

    C sitting on a beam with a leg either side

    D making progress along the length of a beam

6. In stanza 2 the writer says: Their homage rises without a sound
This implies the spectators

    A are thinking about going home
    B are oblivious of the city noises
    C are not interested in the dogman
    D watch in silent admiration

7. In the poem the words *arrayed in far-off random files* implies that the people are

    A in a far-off fixed formation
    B trapped well below on the ground
    C forming tight, little groups
    D lining up to form a queue

8. What do the spectators faces look like from the dogman's location?
Write your answer on the line. _____

Understanding Year 6 Comprehension
A. Horsfield © Five Senses Education © W. Marlin

Interviewer: Describe this work, *Fish are gold*.

TH: This painting was created to show the fragility of the oceans. It is intended to provoke thought on what could happen if the eco-system is damaged. Often first signs of an unbalanced eco-system are seen in oceans and waterways. It won an environment prize. Fish are gold took about three months to paint. It was an experiment to challenge my ability in a new medium I had only just began to use.

In: When did you know you had a talent for illustration?

TH: I began painting and drawing before I started school. I thought my paintings were neater and better executed than the efforts of other kids.

In: Who or what has influenced or inspired your work?

TH: I was inspired by the colours I saw—and the smells of the paper in newsagents! My favourite artist is Brett Whitely. His style was everything I don't do. His work is more carefree, more open.

In: Have you ever studied your craft at an institution of any sort?

TH: I studied up to the end of secondary school at Frensham, where I had private art lessons as well as regular art classes.

In: Do you have to wait for a flash of inspiration?

TH: Much of it comes from the natural environment—patterns in nature and reflections.

In: What is your favourite media and subjects for creating pictures?

TH: I began with watercolours but I now use anything I can think of.

In: Describe your studio and its advantages/disadvantages.

TH: My studio is at Crescent Head (NSW). It is light and airy and has views of the beach and ocean. It helps me to relax.

In: What are you working on at the moment?

TH: A collage of torn tissue paper and acrylics on canvas. It's a piece with a little more artistic licence than some of my earlier work.

In: What successes have you had as an artist?

TH: I have had quite a few sales, won cash prizes and been awarded commendations certificates at art shows. This is having a snowball effect on my career.

In: What's the worst thing about being a freelance artist?

TH: Getting exposure for my works, time transporting pictures to exhibitions and the cost of framing!

In: What advice do you have to budding artists?

TH: Don't procrastinate. Have a space to be artistic whenever you like.

In: Thank you Trudy.

Understanding Interviews

Circle a letter or write an answer for questions 1 to 8.

1. How long did it take the artist to finish *Fish are gold*?
   - A several years
   - B the time she spent at primary school
   - C about three months
   - D her time at private high school classes

2. When did Trudy's interest in art begin?
   - A before she started school
   - B at primary school
   - C when at Frensham school
   - D after arriving at Crescent Head

3. What does Trudy find most costly about making a living from art?
   - A the fees to enter art competitions
   - B the charges involved in framing her art
   - C the expense in hanging her works at exhibitions
   - D the cost of transporting her works to galleries

4. What word from the text means to postpone or put off doing something?
   Write your answer in the line. _____

5. To the last question Trudy offers advice for *budding artists*.
   A *budding artist* is one who
   - A is just starting to succeed
   - B needs time to get started in painting
   - C finds a reason to take up art
   - D is a novice at painting

6. What is the motivation behind Trudy's painting, *Fish are gold*?
   - A the importance of winning a financial prize
   - B to create works like those of Brett Whitely
   - C a concern for the environment
   - D to support those who have helped develop her skills

7. Which word best describes Trudy's present artistic style?
   - A photographic   B experimental   C conventional   D commercial

8. What is the name given to an artist's work space?
   - A office   B workshop   C study   D studio

Lit Tip 25 – Improve your literacy skills   Person for pronouns (revision)

Person is a feature of personal pronouns (see **Lit Tip 11**) and nouns.
Simply stated **first person** refers to the person speaking (me, I).
Second person refers to the person spoken to (you) and **third person** refers to the person spoken about (he, she it them). Writers use **person** to create a style of writing.

Indicate whether the nouns or the pronouns are first second or third (1, 2 or 3) person.

1. Will you (   ) give it (   ) to Marcia (   )?.   2. You (   ) and I (   ) can carry the food.

3. Most of the TH's responses in the above interview are in _____ person.

4. Most of the questions asked in the above interview are in _____ person.

Understanding Year 6 Comprehension
A. Horsfield © Five Senses Education © W. Marlin

Proper Nouns to Common Nouns

Many of the words that are used in everyday English were once the names of people or places.

A word that comes from a person's name is called an EPONYM and if it comes from a place name it is called a TOPONYM. It is not necessary to remember these names to be intrigued by the origins of some everyday words.

Eponyms and toponyms come into the language from various sources, such as:

- real people
- places where something occurred (real or fictional)
- folk stories (myths, legends)
- the arts (literature, theatre, music)

Here are examples from each of the above categories.

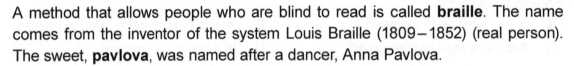

A method that allows people who are blind to read is called **braille**. The name comes from the inventor of the system Louis Braille (1809–1852) (real person). The sweet, **pavlova**, was named after a dancer, Anna Pavlova.

A bubbly wine drink that originated in the Champagne district of France is often called **champagne** (real place). Household linen, **manchester**, was first factory produced in the city of Manchester.

When a sound is reflected off valley walls we call it an **echo**. Echo was a mountain nymph in a Greek legend. Her chattering annoyed the gods so much that she was put under a spell only to utter the last words spoken to her (myth).

The word **utopia** is used to describe an ideal place. It comes from a book written by Sir Thomas Moore in 1516 called Utopia (literature).

The change from a proper noun to a common noun is not immediate. In 1938 Laszlo Biro invented the ball-point pen. Many companies began to produce ball-point pens but they were all generally referred to as being **biros**.

The **mackintosh** (often abbreviated to mac or mack) is a form of waterproof raincoat first sold in 1824, made out of rubberised fabric. It is named after the Scottish inventor Charles Macintosh.

Here are a few you might like to check out: japan, spartan, marathon, banksia.

Source: http://en.wikipedia.org/wiki/Mackintosh

1. According to the text, over a period of time some proper nouns may

   A   become common nouns   B   be considered meaningless

   C   be regarded as slang   D   be used as words of ridicule

2. The common noun, utopia, comes from

   A   a place name in a work of fiction   B   the name of a European race

   C   a Greek myth   D   the surname of a real person

3. Which common noun had its origin as the name of a real person?

   A   champagne   B   mackintosh   C   echo   D   manchester

4. A word for the dessert called pavlova had its origin as

   A   an ancient civilization myth   B   a place name

   C   a real person's name   D   the art of dancing

5. A toponym is a word that comes from a

   A   person's name   B   common noun

   C   dessert name   D   place name

6. How did the mountain nymph, Echo, annoy the Greek gods?

   A   She repeated the last words of other people.

   B   She put spells on talkative people.

   C   She was forever chattering.

   D   She interrupted the gods when they were talking.

7. Which of these words has not been used as a common noun?

   A   Biro   B   Buddha   C   Braille   D   Echo

8. Which of these common nouns had its origin as a fictitious place name?

   A.   champagne   B   manchester

   C   pavlova   D   utopia

Lit Tip 26 – Improve your Literacy skills   Eponyms and Toponyms

Can you complete this table? Use any reference material you have available.
The Source refers to its origin. You can be specific. The first one is an example.

Proper noun	Common noun	Meaning	Source
Afghan	afghan	a woollen shawl style used in Afghanistan	place
Diesel			
Vandal			
Atlas			
Aurora			
China			
Scrooge			

How to Cope with Phishing

The definition of phishing (pronounced fishing)is: The fraudulent practice of sending electronic mail (emails) claiming to be from real companies urging individuals to reveal personal information, such as credit-card numbers, online.

The phishing email may look like this:

From: "Spin - ISP (support@spin.net.au)
Date: 13 August 2010 12:06:24 AM AEST
To: undisclosed-recipients:
Subject: Urgent upgrading
Reply-To: webmaster.admin22@ml.lt
Dear client
This message is from your email service centre to all users. We are improving our database and e-mail centre due to unusual activities identified in our email system. We are deleting all e-mail accounts identified to improve and create space for new ones.
You are required to immediately verify your email account via email, confirming their identity. This will prevent your mail account termination during this exercise. To confirm your email identity, you must provide the information requested:
* Username: (........) (required)
* Password : (........)(required)
* Date of Birth: (........) (optional)
* Country or territory: (........) (optional)
        (* = Important details)
Provide all this information completely and correctly otherwise, for security reasons, we may have to disable your account temporarily.

What should I do?

As awareness is key, here are some <u>pointers</u> to keep in mind:

- Your service provider will never send an email requesting your password or login details

- No company should ever request your login details in an email

- If you click on a link in an email and are redirected to a website, always check the address to make sure it is genuine

- If unsure, get in contact with the company directly

- If an email seems suspicious, it almost certainly is

- Be sceptical (better safe than sorry)

- Be mindful of scare tactics — or free offers

Turn the tables on "phishers" by raising awareness. If you discover a phishing attempt forward it onto your server.

Adapted from: text Posted on March 8, 2013 by Chad Branks

Understanding Procedures

Circle a letter to answer questions 1 to 8.

1. On receiving their first phishing email a person's initial reaction is most likely to

   A   send lots of emails   B   ignore the email

   C   comply with the instructions   D   contact their server

2. A phishing email is attempting to get an email receiver to

   A   understand the likelihood of potential digital problems

   B   reveal personal financial access information

   C   advise the email addressee of real threats to their service

   D   provide internet users of unnecessary costly services

3. The writer advises that if an email looks suspicious it is most likely

   A   an email sent to an incorrect address

   B   to be fraudulent

   C   an honest attempt to keep users informed

   D   to be from the email server advising of a service updated

4. The word email is an abbreviation for

   B   emergency mail   C   explanatory email

   C   efficient mail   D   electronic mail

5. What is the best defence against email phishing expeditions?

   A   awareness of the scam   B   closing down the personal computer

   C   getting advice from a bank   D   cancelling all internet payments

6. What is meant by *turn the tables* as used in the text?

   A   change the location of the computer desk

   B   begin a new interest

   C   take advantage of another person's weakness

   D   make someone's plans fail

7. Which word could be used in place of *pointers* as used in the text?

   A   signals   B   cursors   C   suggestions   D   arrows

8. The intention of the sender of the email copy recorded in the text is to

   A   scare the receiver into immediate action

   B   persuade the receiver to act properly

   C   hassle the receiver into deleting all emails

   D   intimidate the receiver into changing servers

Lit Tip 27 – Improve your Literacy skills   **Similar or different?**

The prepositions that follow *similar* and *different* can cause confusion (see **Lit Tip 23**).
What is the correct preposition to follow *similar*? We say similar to.
For *different* we say *different from*. It is not generally accepted to say **different than**.
Complete these sentences with the correct preposition.

1. Our car is different _____ anything else on the road.

2. I have had problems similar _____ yours.

Understanding Year 6 Comprehension
A. Horsfield © Five Senses Education © W. Marlin

Emergency Exit Plan

This house is on a sloping block.

The arrows indicate the escape routes in case of a fire.

The acronym **RACE** is a verbal procedure for initially alerting nearby people and reacting to the emergency.

Remove people from immediate danger, if safe to do so, to an area of safety.

Alert occupants and visitors by activating alarm systems or verbally. Yell "Fire! Fire! Fire!" loudly. Even if the incident is seemingly small, the first priority is to notify someone of the emergency.

Contain / confine the emergency where possible and safe to do so.

Extinguish the fire if safe to do so. If not, evacuate via the nearest safe exit and proceed to your designated Assembly Area.

Australia's primary emergency call service number is Triple Zero (000), which can be dialled from any fixed or mobile phone, pay phones and certain Voice over Internet Protocol (VoIP) services.

Source: http://www.ezblueprint.com/examples.htmlReference: http://www.triplezero.gov.au/Pages/Usingotheremergencynumbers.aspx

Understanding Procedures   Circle a letter or write an answer for questions 1 to 8.

1. Which person has two quick escape routes if there is a fire emergency?
     A   Paul   B   Jill   C   the parents   D   a guest

2. If you discover a fire in your home you should immediately yell
     A   "Help! Help!"   B   "Ring Triple Zero!"
     C   "Fire! Fire! Fire!"   D   "Emergency! Emergency!"

3. In which room of the house is there **NO** fire detector?
     A   Bathroom   B   Kitchen
     C   Spare bedroom   D   Parents' bedroom

4. The control to shut off the electricity is
     A   in the bathroom   B   on the deck
     C   beside the kitchen   D   at the back of the garage

5. The fire extinguisher is
     A   near the garage door   B   on the back deck
     C   in the parents' bedroom   D   in the kitchen

6. The word *incident*, as used in the text, means
     A   an illegal act
     B   something that happens
     C   a major disaster
     D   an adventure

7. What does **E** stand for in the acronym **RACE**?
     Write your answer on the line. _____

8. Where would be the best place to display this emergency floor plan in a family home?
     A   near a garage fire extinguisher
     B   on an escape route
     C   in an easily seen position in the kitchen
     D   on the door inside the bathroom

Lit Tip 28 – Improve your Literacy skills   **Plurals for acronyms**

Acronyms and initials (see **Lit Tip 21**) representing nouns can have a plural form.

Examples: one UFO or many UFOs, one ATM or many ATMs.
There is a tendency for some people to make the s an apostrophe s ('s).
UFO's and ATM's are **incorrect**.
Write the plural for these. 1. IMB _____ 2. PIN _____

Years are treated the same way. It is 1990s **not** 1990's.

Look at **Text 21** again. The years for which decade are recorded there? _____

Understanding Year 6 Comprehension
A. Horsfield © Five Senses Education © W. Marlin

29 Read the narrative *The Lady in Black.*

The Lady in Black

Winter. One in the morning.

Night has leeched life from the suburbs on the surrounding hills and from the wharves around the backwater. <u>The bus is a vulnerable glow-worm</u> of light crawling along the wet, black road.

Brett stares absent-mindedly through the window glare into the damp gloom. All he can see is the pool of yellow light racing along the road as if accompanying the bus on its silent mission. The road could well be the black surface of still water of the nearby bay. The scattered lights of the city centre are lost in the cold mist that drifts across the water and seeps into the surrounding locked suburbs.

The bus stops for T-intersection lights that carry on their relentless cycle of amber, red, green, amber, red, green though the bus is the only traffic at this hour. It could be a ghost town. Brett stares out into the bushes growing along the roadside. A sign states that the landscaping is a government project to green the environment.

Behind the saplings and bushes are the vague skeletal structures of a silent railway goods yard. Brett shivers and thinks how great it will be to get into bed. Selling hamburgers on the late night shift was not a great challenge but it gave him some holiday cash.

The bus shudders gently forward as the lights flash to green.

Out of the corner of his eye Brett catches sight of a movement in a gap in the shrubbery.

For a moment he thinks it his reflection in the lightly misted glass. He hadn't seen the woman in black until she had moved. He almost called out to the driver to stop then abruptly realised she didn't want to catch the bus. It wasn't a regular bus stop.

The image of the woman in a long black shawl and black hat haunts him. What could she be doing there? He tries to dismiss the image from his mind.

Understanding Narratives

1. The lady dressed in black that Brett saw was
   - A in the hamburger cafe
   - B beside bushes by the road way
   - C leaving a railway goods yard
   - D standing under the traffic lights

2. The first line of the extract suggests that the narrative will
   - A be amusing
   - B have a happy ending
   - C have a peaceful setting
   - D introduce a sinister incident

3. The extract is written in
   - A first person
   - B second person
   - C third person

4. The most likely reason the writer repeats the colours *amber, red, green* is to
   - A give a feeling of relentless monotony
   - B provide some colour for the night
   - C demonstrate the importance of traffic lights
   - D stress the lack of control people have over their lives

5. The writer states in paragraph 2 *the bus is a vulnerable glow-worm.*
   The words *the bus is a vulnerable glow-worm* is an example of
   - A a simile
   - B a metaphor
   - C an exaggeration
   - D alliteration

6. What starts Brett thinking about the comforts of his own bedroom?
   - A selling hamburgers on the night shift
   - B a government landscaping sign
   - C the silhouette of a railway goods yard
   - D the lights of the bus along the road

7. The text creates a feeling of
   - A foreboding
   - B relief
   - C anxiety
   - D desperation

8. The bus stopped because
   - A Brett had called for the driver to stop
   - B it was a regular bus stop
   - C a person had signalled the bus to stop
   - D the traffic lights had changed to red

Lit Tip 29 – Improve your Literacy skills   Adding ing to -ic words

A number of *ic* ending words can take an *ing* suffix – but there is a catch!
It someone goes on a picnic we can say they are picnicking.
Did you see the *k* sneak in after the *c*?
This happens with many *ic* ending words: mimic - mimicking, frolic - frolicking
Using the same rule add *ing* to these words.

traffic _____, politic _____, panic _____

Understanding Year 6 Comprehension
A. Horsfield © Five Senses Education © W. Marlin

Bubonic Plague Hits Queensland

> Bubonic plague: A contagious, often fatal epidemic disease caused by the bacterium *Yersinia pestis*, transmitted from person to person or by the bite of fleas from an infected host, especially a rat, and characterized by chills, fever, vomiting, diarrhoea, and the swelling of certain glands.

In April 1900 the Adelaide Steamship Company's ship Cintra arrived in Townsville carrying a sick steward.

A local doctor by the name of Ernest Humphry diagnosed the steward with bubonic plague. In the Middle Ages, bubonic plague wiped out between one-third and one-half of the population of Europe. Fleas on plague-carrying rats spread the disease from port to port via the shipping trade, infecting coastal towns the world over.

Adelaide Steamship Company Wharf, Townsville c.1990 City Libraries Local History Collection

In Townsville, the Cintra's passengers and crew were quarantined at West Point on Magnetic Island, but with a bustling port in the heart of the city it wasn't long before cases of plague were reported on the mainland.

A temporary plague hospital was hastily built on the Town Common, to treat plague victims and to isolate their immediate contacts. Despite the obvious threat the plague posed to the community, strict government quarantine regulations which were designed to limit the spread of bubonic plague, were met with ridicule in Townsville.

Many local residents were doubtful as to whether the illness was really bubonic plague. Some people felt justified in ignoring the quarantine regulations.

In September a furore erupted over the regulations when Henry Cockerill, the father of a 25-year old blacksmith infected with bubonic plague, refused to allow his son to be taken away to the plague hospital.

Two doctors attempted to forcibly remove the patient, but a crowd of 400 onlookers assembled at the Lamington Road residence, creating something akin to a siege in the West End street.

The crowd shouted their support for Mr Cockerill as he stood steadfastly in the doorway of his home. They jeered at the doctors who were trying to take his son away.

Mr Cockerill sent for Dr Bacot, who had previously treated his son for a broken leg, but because of the quarantine regulations, police wouldn't allow him to enter the house. Eventually, the doctors and ambulance cart went home with the standoff unresolved.

Henry Cockerill Jnr remained quarantined in his own home for ten days under the guard of four police constables.

Thanks to: Trisha Fielding for making this text available, Adapted from: Bulletin Townsvilleeye April 5 2014 p.19
http://northqueenslandhistory.blogspot.com.au/2014/04/bubonic-plague-standoff.html
http://dictionary.reference.com/browse/bubonic+plague

Understanding Newspaper Reports

Circle a letter to answer questions 1 to 8.

1. The first person reported to have bubonic plague in Townsville was
   - A Henry Cockerill Jnr
   - B Dr Ernest Humphry
   - C Henry Cockerill
   - D a ship's steward

2. When a case of Bubonic plague was discovered on the ship *Cintra,* the passengers and crew were
   - A not allowed to leave the ship
   - B assembled at the Lamington Road
   - C quarantined at West Point on Magnetic Island
   - D relocated to a temporary hospital on the Town Common

3. The people of Townsville reacted to the threat of plague
   - A as if it was of no importance
   - B by obeying quarantine regulations
   - C by shifting to Magnetic island
   - D with respect for the local doctors

4. What was one way in which authorities tried to stop the spread of bubonic plague?
   - A letting victims recover at home
   - B banning ships entering Townsville
   - C isolating immediate contacts
   - D providing guards for victims

5. What order is usually generally given to points written in a newspaper report?
   - A the most important points come first
   - B a chronological order of events
   - C a random sampling of interesting topics
   - D scientific facts precede public opinion

6. How can the crowd that shouted their support for Mr Cockerill be described?
   - A They knew more than the officials.
   - B They wanted to contain the spread of the disease.
   - C They believed the plague had been eliminated from Australian soil.
   - D They were ignorant of plague facts.

7. A suitable synonym to *akin* (to) as used in the text (third last paragraph) would be
   - A similar
   - B near
   - C parallel
   - D relative

8. What happened to Henry Cockerill Jnr?
   - A He was treated for plague by Dr Bacot.
   - B He was kept under guard in his own home.
   - C He was finally removed to a hospital by two doctors.
   - D He was found to be free of bubonic plague.

Lit Tip 30 – Improve your Literacy skills   **Correct usage: opposite**

Which word should follow opposite? The opposite _____ wet is dry. *to, from* or *of*?
The correct word is *of* – the opposite *of* wet.
To is not necessary in this sentence: The bank is opposite (to) the Post Office.
Opposite can be an adjective (opposite team), noun (the opposite of), adverb (the shop opposite), or preposition (sat opposite one another).
What part of speech is *opposite* in these sentences?

1. The opposite of hot is cold. _____   2. We walked in opposite directions. _____

Understanding Year 6 Comprehension
A. Horsfield © Five Senses Education © W. Marlin

Cua Van Village

Cua Van Village has a population of over 700 in around 200 households. They mainly earn their livelihood by fishing. So what's so special about Cua Van village in Vietnam?

Answer. This World Heritage listed village actually floats on the water of Halong Bay.

Inhabitants almost entirely live in a commune of floating houses and boats, earning a living by fish-catching and aquaculture - floating fish farms. It is one of many villages in the bay. In Halong Bay traditional cultural values are well preserved.

The name, Halong Bay, literally means descending dragon bay. The bay features thousands of limestone outcrops, and spires and isles in various sizes and shapes called a karst landscape. The limestone has gone through 500 million years of formation in different conditions and environments. The evolution of the bay has taken 20 million years and is the result of the tropical wet climate.

The climate of the bay is tropical, wet, sea islands, with two seasons - hot and moist summers, and dry and cold winters.

Photo 1

Photo 2

The floating houses under the limestone cliffs are spacious and clean. Most families have basic household furniture with radios and TVs. Some houses have tiled roofs.

The village boasts a floating clinic, floating police station and floating school for their children with four classrooms and one small room for teachers. Cua Van school has 7 classes, mainly in grade 1 and grade 2. The youngest pupils are about 8, while the oldest are maybe in their mid teens.

Children begin rowing from an early age. When they reach school age many have to row to school. Their bustling calling and their flopping rowing liven up the atmosphere of the quite bay. The grocery store is a rowing boat. It travels around the village selling basic household supplies.

The bay around Cua Van is kept clean and litter free. People take turns collecting waste from their marine environment.

Sources:
http://www.monkeyislandresort.com/surrounding/cua-van-floating-village-between-halong-bay-and-lan-ha-bayhtml
http://www.vspiritcruises.com/halong-bay-attractions/halong-bay-fishing-villages/cua-van-fishing-village/
http://www.vietnamwiki.net/Ha_Long-Overview-Ha_Long_Bay-P130

1. What is so interesting about Cua Van Village?

    A   It is in a bay full of limestone spires and outcrops.

    B   It is located in a bay described as *descending dragon* bay.

    C   The waters by Cua Van village are kept clean by the villagers.

    D   The village buildings float on the water of Halong Bay.

2. About how many homes are in Cua Van village?

    A   200   B   500   C   700   D   900

3. Look at Photo 1. Why would this very young child be rowing this boat?

    A   The man is too tired to be rowing.

    B   The child is making his way to school.

    C   The child is learning the skills to survive in Cua Van.

    D   The boat is being used as a plaything.

4. The people of the Cua Van village live in a *commune* (see paragraph 2).
    A commune lifestyle is one where

    A   children have to help out   B   the basic needs of life are limited

    C   cooperation is important   D   groceries are delivered by boat

5. Which of these places is **unlikely** to be found floating in Cua Van village?

    A   fish farm   B   supermarket

    C   school   D   police station

6. Which of the options indicates that Cua Van village is of significance?

    A   a World Heritage listing   B   the karst landscape

    C   fish-catching and aquaculture   D   the meaning of the name Halong Bay

7. Which word (paragraph 1) has the meaning of: *a way of getting the necessities of life*
    Write your answer on the line._____

8. According to information in the text the people of Cua Van are

    A   living in primitive conditions   B   very responsive to their environment

    C   looking for a safer place to live D   embarrassed by their life style

---

Lit Tip 31 – Improve your Literacy skills   Commas in series (paired words)

Commas in single word series are simple: I had red, blue, pink *and* green pens.
The comma goes after each item in the series except when *and* is used between the last two items.
Items can be double word items: <u>Old men</u>, <u>happy boys</u> *and* <u>young fathers</u> cheered.
Items can be paired with and. Look at this example:
<u>Cups and saucers</u>, <u>knives and forks</u> *and* <u>bread and butter</u> were taken on the picnic.

Add commas to this sentence.
Uncles and aunts nieces and nephews and close neighbours went to the fair.

Understanding Year 6 Comprehension
A. Horsfield © Five Senses Education © W. Marlin

Twilight Walk

It was early evening on Saturday and the suburban street was nearly deserted. The occasional slow moving car worked its way over the speed humps and around the traffic calmers. A young man, no more than a teenager, on his own, walked purposely down the street then turned to the entrance path of a park. For a moment he seemed to hesitate as if pondering a decision.

Although the path wound its way through the centre of a shadowy park, it was partially lit by sparsely spaced orange lights. The trees hadn't yet lost their autumn leaves and there were pockets of dimness. Further out from the path the shadows were like deep, black holes into the unknown.

A lonesome dog howled in the distance.

A cool breeze wafted briefly and a few leaves flittered to the path as the walker turned into the park picking up speed as he went. About twenty metres in he broke into an easy trot. He quickly glanced behind as he reached the first light. His elongated shadow disappeared into the darkness of the path ahead.

A truck growled down the street but its noise was muffled by the trees and thick shrubs. All the teenager could hear was the sound of his joggers rhythmically scrunching the loose gravel on the asphalt path. He adjusted his breathing to that of his paces. He did a slow, soft count of his steps as if to provide a focus for this effort.

The next light was around a curve in the path. As he moved closer to the light his reforming shadow was behind him.

From the corner of his eye he saw a single shadow move from the bushes further down the path. Unlike the wavering trees this shadow had definition. It moved to the centre of the path and stopped. The teenager quickly glanced back over his shoulder almost stumbling as he did so.

When he righted himself the single shadow had become three.

Understanding Descriptions

Circle a letter to answer questions 1 to 8.

1. This description is most likely from a
   - A newspaper recount
   - B procedure for joggers
   - C fictional narrative
   - D report on park dangers

2. What is the reason the teenager almost stumbled?
   - A he tried to look over his shoulder
   - B he was watching his feet
   - C he was distracted by traffic noise
   - D he was too busy counting

3. What is the most likely reason the teenager looked back over his shoulder?
   - A he expected to have company
   - B he was checking to see if he was being followed
   - C he thought a truck might be following him down the path
   - D he wondered what was happening to his shadow

4. In which order did incidents from the passage happen?
   - **1** a dog's howl was heard in the distance
   - **2** the teenager paused at the park entrance
   - **3** three shadows emerged onto the path
   - **4** the teenager began counting his paces
   - A **2, 1, 4, 3**
   - B **1, 4, 3, 2**
   - C **1, 4, 3, 2**
   - D **2, 1, 3, 4**

5. What first made the teenager aware that something might be amiss?
   - A a dog howling in the distance
   - B the changing shadows his body made as he jogged
   - C leaves falling from the trees along the pathway
   - D a shadow which appeared to have solid form

6. The text creates the feeling that
   - A the teenager is about to meet old friends
   - B something sinister will happen
   - C the park is a peaceful place
   - D the teenager has everything under control

7. Which word best describes how the jogger was feeling as he entered the park?
   - A agitated
   - B assured
   - C defiant
   - D apprehensive

8. A more intriguing and appropriate title for the passage would be
   - A Shadowy Park
   - B Ambush
   - C Lonely Dog
   - D The Jogger

Lit Tip 32 – Improve your Literacy skills   Should have / of

People who say or write *should of* are making a mistake. The correct grammar is *should have* which is often abbreviated to *should've*. The *ve* can be mistaken for of.
Should have is a two-word verb for referring to the past event that did not happen.
Of is a preposition. (**Don't ever use** off of. Example: It fell off of the truck.)
Read these sentences softly to yourself. Pronounce the words carefully.

Jack should have gone home.   Jack should've gone home.

Jill could have helped but she was busy.   Jill could've helped but she was busy.

I would have replied but I was sick.   I would've replied but I was sick.

Understanding Year 6 Comprehension
A. Horsfield © Five Senses Education © W. Marlin

33 Read the book review *Tales of a Fourth Grade Nothing.*

Tales of a Fourth Grade Nothing

What parents need to know:
Educational value 2/5
Positive role models 4/5
Violence 1/5

Parents need to know that Tales of a Fourth Grade Nothing is the first in Judy Blume's "Fudge" series about the Hatcher family: Mr and Mrs Hatcher, their older son Peter, and younger son Farley Drexel, whom everyone calls Fudge.

The novel takes a humorous but honest view of <u>brother rivalry</u>, and the challenges of reasoning with an imaginative, stubborn 3-year-old. Fudge's <u>antics</u> annoy his brother and sometimes land him in precarious situations, but Fudge will amuse middle-grade readers. Fudge hurts himself in one incident, bleeding and losing a couple of baby teeth, and he is hospitalised after eating a non-food item. Kids might be slightly alarmed by these situations or by adults sometimes losing their tempers (verbally), but the book's humorous tone keeps things light. Mrs Hatcher says her husband doesn't know much about caring for children, and he doesn't know how to cook a meal.

Parent's reaction:

A terrific read. Toddler's antics annoy his brother but amuse readers. Gender roles are indeed out-dated, but children and parents need to know that this book was written in 1972, when understanding of gender roles was just starting to change. Aside from that, children, especially those with siblings who are several years younger than they are, will notice that Peter's mother seems to care more about Fudge than him, a common perception among children who have siblings younger than 5 or 6. Most children (and adults) who read this book will agree that Peter's father understands him better and seems to treat him better than his mother does. For example, after Fudge goes into Peter's room, the mother refuses to consider buying a lock for the door to Peter's bedroom, but the father thinks otherwise and buys one. As such, they'll like the father better than the mother, as they'll identify more easily with him. As for Peter's problems with Fudge, those problems will bring back memories, both good and bad, to the readers of experiences they've had in their own lives, as they are amusing and funny.

Permission applied for: 17/06/14
Source: www.commonsensemedia.org/book-reviews/tales-of-a-fourth-grade-nothing (adapted)

Understanding Book Reviews

Circle a letter to answer questions 1 to 8.

1. After reading this review how would most parents rate this book for their children?

   A   essential   B   undesirable   C   acceptable   D   average

2. The reviewer treats the violence in the book as

   A   likely to alarm older children
   B   not being very realistic
   C   if it could be distressing to parents
   D   of little importance

3. The title of the book suggests that Peter, an important character in the book,

   A   has a low opinion of himself   B   enjoys fun at the expense of others
   C   behaves mischievously   D   never scored well in school tests

4. Brother rivalry could best be described as the

   A   need brothers have to separate ways of life.
   B   competition and fighting between brothers.
   C   preference parents have for one or the other of the boys.
   D   way brothers have similar interests.

5. What justification does the review have for criticisms of the story?

   A   The author had little understanding of family situations.
   B   The story has valuable educational possibilities.
   C   The brothers' parents are just like most parents.
   D   The story was written in 1972 when there were different social attitudes.

6. How does Blume's story portray the parents, Mr and Mrs Hatcher?

   A   The parents have no respect for their children.
   B   The parents are equally understanding of their children's needs.
   C   The parents' roles are quite out-dated.
   D   The parents are in total agreement as to how to treat their offspring.

7. Which word would be a suitable synonym for *antics* as used in the text?

   A   pranks   B   feats   C   adventures   D   stunts

8. The reviewer's reaction to the violence in the story is

   A   one of alarm   B   one of acceptance
   C   to dismiss it.   D   to treat it as amusing.

Lit Tip 33 – Improve your Literacy skills   Apostrophes for plurals

For singular nouns to show possession you add an apostrophe s ('s), e.g. pig's snout.
Most plural nouns take s then the apostrophe (s'), e.g. parents' car (two parents).
If the spelling changes the rule generally applies, e.g. witches' brooms, ladies' club.
For irregular plurals you add an apostrophe s ('s), e.g. geese's food, men's shed.
Add the correct possessive form to show ownership in these.

mice _____ tails, Dad_____hat, babie_____ milk, women _____ meeting, boy _____ class

Note: When the plural noun is the same as the singular noun you add apostrophe s('s), e.g. sheep's wool, deer's eyes. The context should tell you if it is singular or plural.

Understanding Year 6 Comprehension
A. Horsfield © Five Senses Education © W. Marlin

The Cathedral Fig

The Cathedral Fig is in north Queensland. This fig's name comes from its cathedral-like root formation. The elaborate <u>strangling</u> habits of this tree are common among tropical figs.

Strangling figs start their lives high in the forest <u>canopy</u>. A small seed is dropped onto a branch, crevice or in a plant growing on the tree, by a bird or bat. It then germinates.

The seedling lives in the tree's canopy, obtaining nutrients from leaf litter and rainfall.

When the seedling becomes too large to rely on these nutrients it waits for favourable conditions and then sends out long cable-like roots that descend to the ground. Other roots encircle the host. The fig continues to grow, either outliving its host or killing it by strangulation.

Cathedral Fig facts:

- The tree started as a seed 2 mm in size.
- The tree has a girth of 44 m. If 24 people linked hands around the tree they would just join up.
- The tree could be 500 years old.
- Scientists have estimated the tree to be 48 m high – as high as a five-storey building.
- The crown of the tree extends over 20 000 square metres – the size of two Olympic swimming pools.
- The fig's leaf load is about 1000 kg – the mass of a small car.

A strange relationship

Fig trees and fig wasps have an interesting, interdependent relationship and each species of fig wasp is only able to pollinate the flowers of one species of fig tree.

A tiny female fig wasp (3mm long) is attracted by the smell of the flowers on the developing fig. She deposits her eggs by boring into the flowers. In the process the female wasp pollinates many of the surrounding flowers. When the larvae develop they produce a substance to stop the fig fruit from ripening - ensuring the fruit and larvae are not eaten by bats or birds.

On maturity the wasps emerge after burrowing through the fig wall.

Sources: http://www.nprsr.qld.gov.au/parks/curtain-fig/culture.html
Local information boards.

Understanding Reports

Circle a letter to answer questions 1 to 8.

1. The Cathedral Fig seeds germinate
   - A   along the branches of a host tree
   - B   in a bird's nest
   - C   in nutrients on the ground
   - D   under a host tree

2. The forest canopy is the
   - A   shaded undergrowth of a tree.
   - B   uppermost branches of forest trees.
   - C   growth of plants among the branches of a tree.
   - D   root system that forms an above-ground opening.

3. What is the outcome between a strangler fig and the host tree?
   - A   The fig tree's roots choke the host tree
   - B   The fig tree prevents the host tree from getting enough light
   - C   The host tree continues to provide nutrients for the fig tree
   - D   The two trees live together to the benefit of each other

4. The tree is describes as having *a girth of 44m*.
   The *girth* of a tree a measurement
   - A   up the trunk to the first branch
   - B   beneath the tree's trunk
   - C   through the tree's trunk
   - D   around the trunk

5. The information in **Cathedral Fig facts** is intended to
   - A   make people realise the importance of the tree
   - B   show how the tree depends on bats and birds
   - C   give some idea of the tree's size
   - D   reveal the 500-year history of the tree

6. What deters bats and birds from eating the fruit of the fig tree?
   - A   the presence of wasps
   - B   the difficulty of finding the fruit
   - C   the fear of being strangled
   - D   the lack of ripeness in the fruit

7. What part of speech is the word strangling as used in paragraph 1?
   - A   verb
   - B   adjective
   - C   adverb
   - D   noun

8. Which of these facts is the writer most sure about?
   - A   the age of the tree
   - B   the mass of the tree's leaves
   - C   the length of the girth
   - D   the area covered by the crown

Lit Tip 34 – Improve your Literacy skills   Hyphens

The hyphen's main purpose is to glue words together and prevent confusion.
Hyphens are often used with time ideas: a two-year-old, seven forty-five, mid-July
They are used with fractions: *two-fifths of the students* and with numbers: *forty-one*
As important as hyphens are to clear writing they can become an annoyance if overused. If in doubt, check a dictionary. There are no spaces with hyphens.
Add the hyphen to these.

X ray,   top notch   father in law   sugar free   fifty five   4 bedroom flat

Understanding Year 6 Comprehension
A. Horsfield © Five Senses Education © W. Marlin

What are Janus Words?

Janus words got their name from an ancient Italian deity regarded as the doorkeeper of heaven and is represented as having two faces - at the back and at the front of his head. The month of January is also named after Janus as it stands at the entrance of the new year but can look back on the old year.

Janus words look 'both ways' due to their contradictory meanings. Compare the meanings of the word dust in these two sentences:

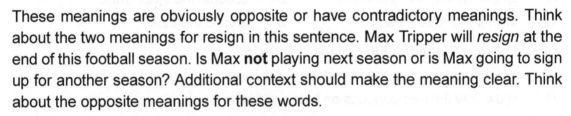

1. Mum told me to dust the hallway table.

2. Many farmers dust their crop with fertilizer.

In example 1. dust means to remove dust.

In example 2. dust means to cover with dust.

These meanings are obviously opposite or have contradictory meanings. Think about the two meanings for resign in this sentence. Max Tripper will *resign* at the end of this football season. Is Max **not** playing next season or is Max going to sign up for another season? Additional context should make the meaning clear. Think about the opposite meanings for these words.

hysterical: **1.** frightened and out of control: **2.** funny

fast: **1.** moving quickly: **2.** unable to move (e.g. a ship held fast on rocks)

weather: **1.** to withstand a storm: **2.** to wear away

screen: **1.** to show, (e.g. a film): **2.** to hide something

Can you see opposite meanings in these sentences?

The British fought with the Russians in a number of wars. (Were they opposing forces **or** were they on the same side?) Our chemist dispenses with accuracy. (Is she very careful when she dispenses **or** she doesn't worry about being careful?)

Words, such as those listed, take on different meanings as a result of usage over time. The word bolt can mean something is firmly fixed, but can equally be applied to someone bounding away. Both meanings emerged from the original use of 'bolt' which was a projectile or missile such as an arrow. It could travel at great speed and because its point could be used to pin something down.

Source: http://blog.oxforddictionaries.com/2012/06/contronyms/ (adapted)

Understanding Explanations

Circle a letter or write an answer for questions 1 to 8.

1. What duty had Janus supposedly performed?
   - A   he named the first month of the year.
   - B   he protected ancient Italians
   - C   he was the doorkeeper of heaven
   - D   he introduced the idea of a new year

2. Trudy said the film was *hysterical*. She had tears in her eyes most of the time. When Trudy describes the film as *hysterical* she means it was
   - A   hilarious   B   sorrowful   C   frightening   D   crazy

3. Janus is called a deity (paragraph 1). What is a deity?
   - A   a type of heavenly guard   B   a person with two faces
   - C   a word with two meanings   D   a supreme being

4. Why are the words 'both ways' (paragraph 2) in inverted commas?
   - A   to help the reader understand the text
   - B   to indicate an unusual use of the words
   - C   to warn readers the words have been used incorrectly
   - D   to show that the writer is unsure of the facts

5. Which sentence uses *screen* to mean to hide something?
   - A   Every window has a screen to keep out flies.
   - B   Health officials screen all visitors to the hospital.
   - C   Marge's hair flung across to screen her face.
   - D   The club will screen a video at their next meeting.

6. Hold up can mean to support or to hinder.
   What does hold up mean in the sentence below?

   Road works will hold up the smooth flow of traffic.

   Write your answer on the line. _____

7. What would be a suitable synonym for *point* as used in the last line?
   - A   tip   B   head   C   direct   D   spot

8. What conclusion can be drawn from the text?
   - A   the meaning of words is fixed
   - B   words have no meaning out of context
   - C   most words have an opposite meaning
   - D   words can assume contradictory meanings over time

Lit Tip 35 – Improve your Literacy skills   **Onomatopoeia**

(Pronounced: ono -mata- **pee** -ah)

Onomatopoeia refers to words that sound like the sound it represents, e.g. frogs <u>croak</u>, sheep <u>baa</u>, cats <u>purr</u> and lemonade <u>fizzes</u>.

Many 'hitting' noises are examples: clank, click, thump, knock, thud

Using onomatopoeia carefully can make your writing more interesting.

Compare: Cars went past the finish line.   Cars zoomed past the finish line.
   Jane fastened her seat belt.   Jane click-clacked her seat belt.

Add suitable 'sound' words for: electric motors _____ , car horns _____

Understanding Year 6 Comprehension
A. Horsfield © Five Senses Education © W. Marlin

The Mt Hypipamee Crater

The Mt Hypipamee Crater is in the Atherton Tablelands west of Cairns (Qld).

The crater is a huge volcanic pipe that was formed by a gaseous explosion that blasted half a million tons of basalt to create a vent hole. The <u>pipe</u> was opened upward through surface rocks by gas produced from molten rock below as a result of tremendous pressure. The vent exploded sending volcanic bombs across the landscape. Angular blocks of granite, as large as refrigerators, are scattered in the nearby rainforest, <u>giving testimony</u> to the power of the explosion that hurled them there.

These volcanic events are associated with the creation of diamonds.

The crater has a diameter of 61m at water level. It is 140m deep including an 80m pool of still water covered in duckweed. It is 60m down to the water level.

The Europeans discovery was accidental when in 1879 a group of gold prospectors almost fell into it.

In 1930 it was decided to name the crater Mount Hypipamee, an aboriginal word associated with local Aboriginal Dreamtime. The name is a corruption of the Aboriginal word, *nabbanabbamee*, which is connected to a legend of two young men who cut down a sacred candlenut tree only to be swallowed up by the crater.

It was thought that the crater was connected to other crater lakes via water tunnels but this has been disproved. It may have originated from Aboriginal Dream time stories. Legend tells of an aboriginal woman that fell into the crater and later surfaced in Lake Eacham - another crater lake.

The crater is not a vertical cylinder but has a submerged passage that turns under the lookout, 80m below the surface. Perch-like fish and small crustaceans live in the water.

The craters of the Atherton area owe their presence to past volcanic activity. The most recent activity was between 10,000 and 20,000 years ago. Dr Lin Sutherland, in *The Volcanic Earth*, maintains that the local volcanic activity is <u>dormant</u> rather than extinct.

Sources: http://en.wikipedia.org/wiki/Mount_Hypipamee_Crater (adapted)

Local information display boards.

Understanding Reports

1. What is unusual about the Hypipamee Crater?
   - A   It is the only crater in the Atherton Tablelands.
   - B   It is connected to other water-filled craters.
   - C   It has a submerged underwater passage.
   - D   It is the crater of an active volcano.

2. What evidence is there that the Mt Hypipamee explosion was a huge explosion?
   - A   the depth of water in the crater hole
   - B   the size of boulders scattered over the area
   - C   the possibility of diamonds being formed
   - D   the legends surrounding the crater's formation

3. How deep is the water in the Hypipamee Crater?
   - A   60m   B   61m   C   80m   D   140m

4. The text states: *The pipe was opened upward through surface rocks*
   What is the pipe the writer referring to?
   - A   a cylindrical hole in the earth   B   an artificial hole in the ground
   - C   metal tubes placed in the water   D   the drainage system for the crater

5. What word of warning does the text contain?
   - A   the crater is a danger to prospectors
   - B   the only way to escape from the crater is to swim out
   - C   hurled rocks are a threat to people in the area
   - D   there could be more volcanic eruptions in the area

6. The name for the Mt Hypipamee crater
   - A   is in memory of the Aboriginal woman who fell into the crater
   - B   is a rough translation of an Aboriginal word
   - C   was given to the crater by early gold prospectors
   - D   describes the unusual formation of the hole

7. The words, *giving testimony*, as used in the text have a similar meaning to
   - A   providing proof   B   making available
   - C   supplying evidence   D   presenting clues

8. An antonym for *dormant* as used in the last paragraph would be
   - A   dangerous   B   asleep   C   risky   D   active

Lit Tip 36 – Improve your Literacy skills   **Correct usage**

It is **wrong** to say
 I am bored <u>of</u>
 I am interested <u>about</u>
 I need help <u>on</u> English

It is **right** to say
 I am bored <u>with</u>
 I am interested <u>in</u>
 I need help <u>with</u> English

Tick the correct usage (you may check with a reference source).
 1. <u>In</u> my point of view   OR   <u>From</u> my point of view
 2. Fred apologised <u>about</u>   OR   Fred apologised <u>for</u>

How to Identify the Keys on a Piano

The first thing you notice on your piano keyboard is the use of 88 black and white keys. The 36 black ones are raised and are set back. Each key on the keyboard represents a musical note. These notes use a very complex naming system — the first seven letters of the alphabet: A-B-C-D-E-F-G!

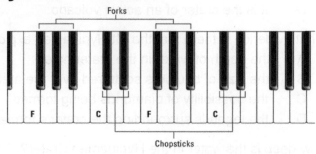

The black keys are in groups of two and three. Think of any set of two black keys as a pair of **chopsticks** and any set of three black keys as the tines on a **fork**. Chopsticks starts with the letter C, and fork starts with the letter F. You can use these chopsticks and forks to help identify the white keys on the keyboard. To the left of the chopsticks (two black keys) is the note C. To the left of the fork (three black keys) is the note F.

Moving up from C you have the notes D, E, F, G. When you get to G, think "Go" as in "go back to the start." The alphabet pattern repeats over and over in octave groupings, which are groups of eight white keys and the black keys between them.

The seven note names (A-B-C-D-E-F-G) are all on the white keys. Black keys represent separate musical notes. The black keys have the same name as the closest white key but with one of the following suffixes:

Sharp is used for a black key to the right of (or higher than) a white key.

Flat is used for a black key to the left of (or lower than) a white key.

Here's another culinary metaphor to help you remember sharps and flats. At your imaginary musical place setting, a white key represents a plate, so:

A *knife is sharp* and lies on the right side of the plate.

A *napkin is flat* and lies on the left side of the plate.

Just remember chopsticks and forks, knives and napkins, and you'll never forget the names of the keys . . . but you may get hungry.

Because each of the black keys lies between two white keys, each black key has two names, depending on the white key you approach it from. For example, the black key to the right of C is C-sharp, but it's also D-flat.

Sources: http://wiki.answers.com/Q/Why_are_piano_keys_black_and_white#ixzz20H34UHmX By Blake Neely

http://www.dummies.com/how-to/content/how-to-identify-the-keys-on-a-piano.html

Understanding Explanations

Circle a letter to answer questions 1 to 8.

1. The information in the text would be useful
- A   for designers of piano keyboards
- B   as a tactic to work out the notes on a keyboard
- C   for people making a living as musicians
- D   as a trick to coax a child to begin piano lessons

2. Tines are part of a
- A   fork
- B   napkin
- C   plate
- D   knife

3. How many black keys are on a common piano keyboard?
- A   8
- B   36
- C   52
- D   88

4. An octave is a
- A   series of two black keys and three black keys
- B   grouping of eight black and white keys
- C   block of eight white keys including their black keys
- D   set of four groups of paired black keys

5. The writer suggests the part of a piano keyboard that can be likened to a fork is
- A   any pair of black keys
- B   the space between the black keys
- C   any set of three black keys
- D   the keys between F and C

6. The writer states: *These notes use a very complex naming system — the first seven letters of the alphabet: A-B-C-D-E-F-G!* (paragraph 1)
By making the claim that the naming is complex the writer is being
- A   cautious
- B   amusing
- C   serious
- D   confusing

7. The writer describes the note on the right of a black key as a
- A   fork
- B   napkin
- C   chopstick
- D   knife

8. The word *culinary* refers to
- A   cooking
- B   crockery
- C   cutlery
- D   china

Lit Tip 37 – Improve your Literacy skills   Characters' names

Choosing the right names for characters in a narrative can be important.
Professional writers choose names carefully and avoid using the names of people they know. Names can go in and out of fashion.
2014 Popular names. Girls: Zoe, Emma, Olivia.   Boys: Aiden, Lucas, Mason

For older characters use names that are now unfashionable: Cedric, Alfred, Doris
Make use of fun names. Ben Down for a cleaner. Rose Thorn for a gardener.
Give two names for elderly characters and two for teenagers.

_____, _____, _____, _____

Understanding Year 6 Comprehension
A. Horsfield © Five Senses Education © W. Marlin

Bellbirds

Bellbirds, by Henry Kendall, is one of Australia's best-loved poems. It captures the cool, dim blue and green of the Australian mountain country. The poem was first published in 1869. Bellbirds (or Bell Miners) are really honeyeaters, closely related to the Noisy Miner.

By channels of coolness their echoes are calling,

And down the dim gorges I hear the creek falling:

It lives in the mountain where moss and the sedges*

Touch with their beauty the banks and the ledges.

Through breaks of the cedar and sycamore bowers**

Struggles the light that is love to the flowers;

And, softer than slumber, and sweeter than singing,

The notes of the bellbirds are running and ringing.

The silver-voiced bellbirds, the darlings of daytime!

They sing in September their songs of the May-time;

When shadows wax*** strong, and the thunderbolts hurtle,

They hide with their fear in the leaves of the myrtle;

When rain and the sunbeams shine mingled together,

They start up like fairies that follow fair weather;

And straightway the hues of their feathers unfolden|

Are the green and the purple, the blue and the golden.

Henry Kendall (1839 - 1882)

* sedges = grass like plants
** bowers = shady places
*** wax = grow

Understanding Poetry

Circle a letter to answer questions 1 to 8.

1. What creates fear in the bellbirds?
   - A deep gorges
   - B thunderbolts
   - C breaks in the cedar
   - D hearing the creeks falling

2. Henry Kendall, the poet, finds the song notes of the bellbirds
   - A harsh
   - B annoying
   - C exciting
   - D soothing

3. Which text from the poem is an example of alliteration? (See Lit Tip 20)
   - A running and ringing
   - B moss and sedges
   - C echoes are calling
   - D thunderbolts hurtle

4. The first stanza of the poem is mainly
   - A a short story about bellbirds
   - B an explanation of bellbird behaviour
   - C a description of the bellbirds' habitat
   - D a plea to protect bellbirds

5. The poet uses these words in the second stanza:
   When rain and the sunbeams shine mingled together
   What is the poet referring to in this line?
   - A a sun shower
   - B a sudden storm
   - C fairy weather
   - D thunder and lightning

6. Which text from the poem is an example of a simile?
   - A the darlings of daytime
   - B the silver-voiced bellbirds
   - C I hear the creek falling
   - D they start up like fairies

7. Where do bellbirds hide to escape danger?
   - A through breaks in the cedar
   - B in the leaves of myrtle trees
   - C down in dim gorges
   - D amongst the moss and the sedges

8. Brackets are used in the introductory boxed text: (or Bell Miners).
   The writer has used brackets to
   - A save writing another sentence
   - B make a correction
   - C give the bellbirds' alternative name
   - D demonstrate his knowledge

Lit Tip 38 – Improve your Literacy skills   Italics

Italics is a sloping typeface. Limited use of italics can add flair to your writing.
It can help readers draw meaning from text.
Italics is used in a variety of written text situations: for the title of created work (*Bellbirds*); for foreign words and scientific words (*carbon dioxide* (CO2)); when referring to specific words (*Eight* and *ate* sound the same) and to add emphasise or contrast to a word (Jim wasn't the *only* boy at church.).
Underline the words that could be in italics in these sentences.

1. I just finished reading Frankenstein.
2. I said funny instead of furry!
3. Homo sapiens is the name given to the human species.
4. I cannot believe Justin ate the whole pie!

Understanding Year 6 Comprehension
A. Horsfield © Five Senses Education © W. Marlin

Eyre's Journey Across the Great Australian Bight

Edward John Eyre came to Australia in 1832 when he was seventeen. Eyre's truly remarkable crossing of The Great Australian Bight and the Nullarbor Plain is the feat for which he is best remembered. His 1839 attempt to reach the centre of the continent failed.

Eyre's route
Eucla
Fowlers Bay
Great Australian Bight
Adelaide
Albany
Spencer Gulf

In 1840 an expedition was being set up to find a route from Adelaide to Albany. Eyre was made leader of the expedition. The group consisted of 6 Europeans and 3 Aborigines, including his friend Wylie. They took 13 horses, 40 sheep and supplies for three months. A government ship was to meet them at Spencer Gulf with supplies.

They set off in November 1840 and followed the coastline west. It was hard going and they found little water along the way. At Fowler's Bay, Eyre decided to send some of the group back to Adelaide and to continue with a small group: his friends Baxter and Wylie, and the other Aborigines. They took 11 horses and 6 sheep.

There were no trees for shelter across the Nullarbor Plain and the heat was intense. They kept to the coastline, but could not reach the sea because of the high cliffs. There was little water. Local Aborigines who showed them where to dig for water saved them. They found some Aboriginal wells at the place now known as Eucla.

From Eucla they could keep close to the beach. Water was still scarce. The Aborigines taught them how to break off roots and suck them for moisture. One by one the packhorses were left behind. They used sponges to collect morning dew from plants.

It was now winter, and the night cold was terrible. They had left behind most of their clothing, and guns and ammunition, with the abandoned packhorses. They had travelled about 1200 kilometres, and still had about 1000 more to go.

The two Aborigines rebelled, killed Baxter and took most of the remaining supplies and guns. Wylie and Eyre continued alone, but it was a week before they found water. They killed and ate kangaroos and other wildlife.

Eyre and Wylie finally met a French ship near the shore but 750 horrendous kilometres from their goal. They were able to get some rest. Then they continued to head westward, having been given clothing and supplies. In July 1841, they reached Albany. The journey from Fowler had lasted almost five months.

Sources: http://www.kidcyber.com.au/topics/eyre.htm
http://www.sahistorians.org.au/175/chronology/may/1-may-1839-edward-john-eyre.shtml
http://www.southaustralianhistory.com.au/johneyre.htm

Understanding Recounts

Circle a letter or write an answer for questions 1 to 8.

1. Which two factors made Eyre's journey difficult?
   - A   the speed sheep could walk and a lack of maps
   - B   attack from local Aborigines and the unsuitability of horses
   - C   extreme temperatures and a shortage of water
   - D   the reliability of the supply ship and the rugged terrain

2. How many men were in Eyre's group when it left Adelaide?
   - A   three
   - B   six
   - C   seven
   - D   nine

3. Eyre was unable to get moisture from
   - A   the broken roots of plants
   - B   sources along the beaches
   - C   the morning dew on plants
   - D   Aboriginal wells

4. How long did Eyre's journey from Fowlers Bay to Albany take?
   - A   5 months
   - B   10 months
   - C   one year
   - D   two years

5. Write the numbers 1 to 4 in the boxes to show the correct order in which events occurred in the recount. The first one (1) has been done for you.

☐	Eyre sends some of his expedition group back to Adelaide.
☐	Local Aborigines show Eyre how to find water on the Nullarbor Plain.
1	Eyre begins his journey west to Albany in 1840.
☐	Aborigines kill Baxter and take the guns and the remaining supplies.

6. Other than Eyre, what was left of Eyre's team when it reached Albany?
   - A   two pack horses
   - B   Eyre's trusted friend, Wylie
   - C   two Aborigines
   - D   Eyre's companion, Baxter

7. Eyre's journey could best be described as
   - A   rash
   - B   futile
   - C   arduous
   - D   inspirational

8. According to the text which statement is correct?
   - A   Eyre's last contact with a ship was at west of Eucla.
   - B   The pack horses starved to death.
   - C   All Aboriginal helpers made the journey to Albany.
   - D   Baxter was killed near Fowlers Bay.

Lit Tip 39 – Improve your Literacy skills   Abbreviation o' words

You have seen the word *o' clock* but what does *o'* stand for? It is short for *of (the)*.
There are a few words that use the short form of *of*.

Examples: *man o' war* (or man-o'-war) refers to an armed sailing ship or a frigate (bird)
jack o' lantern (jack-o'-lantern), a lantern made from a hollow pumpkin
Back o' Bourke, any remote place;   will o' the wisp, a light that appears over marshes

What is a:

cat-o'-nine-tails? _____ , tam-o'-shanter? _____

Understanding Year 6 Comprehension
A. Horsfield © Five Senses Education © W. Marlin

Bon Voyage

"All aboard?" said the captain.

"All aboard, sir!" said the mate.

"Then <u>stand by to let her go</u>."

It was nine o'clock on a Wednesday morning. The good ship Spartan was lying off Boston Quay with her cargo under hatches, her passengers shipped, and everything prepared for a start. The warning whistle had been sounded twice; the final bell had been rung. Her bowsprit was turned towards England, and <u>the hiss of escaping steam</u> showed that all was ready for her run of three thousand miles. She strained at the warps that held her like a greyhound at its leash.

I have the misfortune to be a very nervous man. A sedentary literary life has helped to increase the morbid love of solitude which, even in my boyhood, was one of my distinguishing characteristics.

As I stood upon the quarterdeck of the Transatlantic steamer, I bitterly cursed the necessity which drove me back to the land of my forefathers. The shouts of the sailors, the rattle of the cordage, the farewells of my fellow-passengers, and the cheers of the mob, each and all jarred upon my sensitive nature. I felt sad too. An indescribable feeling, as of some impending calamity, seemed to haunt me. The sea was calm, and the breeze light, yet I felt as if I stood upon the verge of a great though indefinable danger.

I certainly felt far from happy as I threaded my way among the weeping, cheering group of well-wishers which dotted the decks of the Spartan. Had I known the experience which awaited me in the course of the next twelve hours I should even then at the last moment have sprung upon the shore, and made my escape from the accursed vessel.

"Time's up!" said the captain, closing his chronometer with a snap, and replacing it in his pocket.

"Time's up!" said the mate.

There was a last wail from the whistle, a rush of friends and relatives down the gangway. One rope was loosened, the gangway was being pushed away, when there was a shout from the bridge, and two men appeared, running rapidly down the quay. They were waving their hands and making frantic gestures, _____(6)_____ .

From :That Little Square Box by Sir Arthur Conan Doyle
http://ebooks.adelaide.edu.au/d/doyle/arthur_conan/captain/chapter5.html#chapter5

Understanding Narratives

Circle a letter to answer questions 1 to 8.

1. The narrator was on the ship because he was

   A   returning to England

   B   seeing relatives off on a voyage

   C   a friend of the captain   D   meeting his father

2. Who was the first person to see two men rushing towards the ship?

   A   the ship's captain

   B   relatives of the passengers

   C   a person on the bridge

   D   the narrator

3. The writer has used the words: *the hiss of escaping steam*
   The word *hiss* is an example of

   A   alliteration

   B   an interjection

   C   a simile

   D   onomatopoeia

4. The captain says: *stand by to let her go.*
   When the captain says *her* he is referring to

   A   a passenger

   B   the cruise ship

   C   a well-wisher

   D   the gangway

5. The narrator was reacting to the prospect of the voyage to England with a

   A   feeling of excitement

   B   pang of disappointment

   C   degree of apprehension

   D   sense of achievement

6. The final words have been deleted from the text.
   Which words would be best suited to complete the text (6)?

   A   as the captain ordered the mate to drop anchor

   B   apparently with the intention of stopping the ship

   C   while the passengers on deck cheered

   D   just as the police rounded the corner

7. What person is the text written in? (See **Lit Tip 11**)

   A   first person   B   second person   C   third person

8. An alternate suitable title for the text would be

   A   Warning whistles

   B   The good ship Spartan

   C   All aboard!

   D   Anxious departure

Lit Tip 40 – Improve your Literacy skills   **Correct words**

Circle the correct words to complete these sentences.

1. Jack (?) go to the shop.	A hasta	B has to	C haster	D hafta
2. I'm (?) get some money.	A gunna	B gonna	C goana	D going to
3. I'm happy (?) I won a race.	A cause	B acourse	C corser	D because
4. You (?) allowed to go!	A are not	B aint	C isn't	D aunt
5. Max wore (?) muddy shoes.	A his	B hees	C hese	D he's

Understanding Year 6 Comprehension
A. Horsfield © Five Senses Education © W. Marlin

SOLUTIONS

ANSWERS – Reading Comprehension Tests   84, 85

ANSWERS – Literacy Tip Exercises   86, 87

Understanding Year 6 Comprehension
A. Horsfield © Five Senses Education © W. Marlin

Answers — Year 6 Comprehension Questions

No.   Title   Answers

1. Cat V Plant: 1. C   2. B   3. D   4. C   5. A   6. C   7. B   8. A

2. The Blob: 1. A   2. C   3. A   4. B   5. D   6. C   7. D   8. A

3. Paperbark Creek: 1. B   2. D   3. FALSE   4. A   5. B   6. C   7. D   8. A

4. Wasp Attack: 1. C   2. don   3. B   4. D   5. A   6. C   7. D   8. C

5. What is Art Deco?: 1. A   2. B   3. C   4. D   5. C   6. A   7. streamlining   8. D

6. How to Grow Sprouts: 1. C   2. B   3. D   4. A   5. (3, 2, 4, 1)   6. D   7. C   8. A

7. Families Connected?: 1. C   2. A   3. B   4. D   5. B   6. C   7. A   8. D

8. Lombok Floating Palace: 1. D   2. FALSE   3. D   4. B   5. C   6. (2, 4, 3, 1)   7. B   8. A

9. Vietnamese Legend: 1. D   2. C   3. (2)   4. A   5. C   6. B   7. C   8. D

10. The Family Tree: 1. B   2. A   3. D   4. B   5. B   6. NO   7. D   8. C

11. The Ballyhooley Steam Train: 1. D   2. B   3. A   4. C   5. D   6. C   7. B   8. D

12. Rickshaw Rides: 1. D   2. A   3. D   4. B   5. C   6. A   7. B   8. C

13. Footsteps in the Sand: 1. D   2. B   3. feel   4. D   5. C   6. A   7. A   8. C

14. Lone Dog: 1. C   2. A   3. B   4. bide   5. D   6. A   7. B   8. D

15. Traffic Gridlock: 1. A   2. B   3. D   4. C   5. B   6. C   7. A   8. D

16. Forbidden Billabong: 1. D   2. C   3. A   4. B   5. A   6. D   7. C   8. B

17. Duesenberg Automobile: 1. A   2. C   3. A   4. (3, 1, 2, 4)   5. D   6. B   7. C   8. D

18. Interjections: 1. B   2. TRUE   3. A   4. D   5. C   6. A   7. B   8. D

19. Poochera Ants: 1. A   2. B   3. D   4. C   5. B   6. A   7. C   8. B

20. Treasure Island: 1. B   2. A   3. buccaneers   4. D   5. C   6. C   7. A   8. B

Continued on the next page…

No.	Title	Answers

21. Film Review: 1. 3   2. B   3. D   4. A   5. C   6. A   7. B   8. C

22. Storm Surges: 1. cyclones, high tides   2. A   3. B   4. C   5. A   6. D   7. B   8. D

23. Fjords and Sounds: 1. sound   2. B   3. A   4. C   5. D   6. C   7. A   8. B

24. The Dogman: 1. C   2. A   3. D   4. A   5. B   6. D   7. A   8. daisies

25. Artist Interview: 1. C   2. A   3. B   4. procrastinate   5. A   6. C   7. B   8. D

26. Proper Nouns to Common Nouns: 1. A   2. A   3. B   4. C   5. D   6. C   7. B   8. D

27. How to Cope with Phishing: 1. C   2. B   3. B   4. D   5. A   6. D   7. C   8. A

28. Emergency Exit Plan: 1. B   2. C   3. A   4. D   5. A   6. B   7. Extinguish   8. C

29. Lady in Black: 1. B   2. D   3. C   4. A   5. B   6. C   7. A   8. D

30. Bubonic Plague in Queensland: 1. D   2. C   3. A   4. C   5. B   6. D   7. A   8. B

31. Cua Van Village: 1. D   2. A   3. C   4. C   5. B   6. A   7. livelihood   8. B

32. Twilight Walk: 1. C   2. A   3. B   4. A   5. D   6. B   7. D   8. B

33. Book Review: 1. C   2. D   3. A   4. B   5. D   6. C   7. A   8. B

34. Cathedral Fig: 1. A   2. B   3. A   4. D   5. C   6. D   7. B   8. C

35. Janus Words: 1. C   2. A   3. D   4. B   5. C   6. hinder   7. A   8. D

36. The Mt Hypipamee Crater: 1. C   2. B   3. C   4. A   5. D   6. B   7. A   8. D

37. How to Identify the Keys on a Piano: 1. B   2. A   3. B   4. C   5. C   6. B   7. D   8. A

38. Bellbirds: 1. B   2. D   3. A   4. C   5. A   6. D   7. B   8. C

39. Eyre's Journey: 1. C   2. D   3. B   4. A   5. (2, 3, 1, 4)   6. B   7. C   8. A

40. Bon Vogage: 1. A   2. C   3. D   4. B   5. C   6. B   7. A   8. D

Understanding Year 6 Comprehension
A. Horsfield © Five Senses Education © W. Marlin

No. Text title	Topic	Answers
1. Cat v Plant:	Plurals for names from initials	B PCs
2. Film Poster:	Better words for went	Examples: bounced, crawled, trotted
3. Paperbark Creek:	Possessive pronouns	1. its, 2. yours, 3. it's
4. Wasp Attack:	Poetry or prose	Yes (blank verse)
5. What is Art Deco?	The ampersand	1. and, 2. &, 3. &
6. How to Grow Sprouts:	What is idiom?	surprise (or even disbelief)
7. Families Connected?	Rhetorical questions	Isn't it strange?
8. Lombok Palace:	The suffix ship	championship, township, ownership
9. Vietnamese Legend:	Noun or verb?	1. V, N, 2. V, N, 3. N, V
10. Family Tree:	Showing, not telling	Examples: pleased, impressed, happy
11. Ballyhooley Train:	Person	second person
12. Rickshaw Rides:	Topic sentences	In the city the traffic is constant.
13. Footsteps in the Sand:	Irregular verbs	drew, had, kept, gave, bit, tore shook, rung
14. Lone Dog:	Better words than ate	Examples: gulped, devoured, gobbled, nibbled
15. Traffic Gridlock:	Words have many meanings	1. book, 2. hail, 3. lemon
16. Forbidden Billabong:	Using And to begin sentences	No response required
17. Duesenberg Auto:	Comparative adjectives	older, oldest, most
18. Interjections:	Interjections	Examples: Wow, Ouch, Hmm, Yuk, A
19. Poochera Ants:	Swearing in text	No response required
20. Treasure Island:	Alliteration	Examples: 1. shiny, 2. straight, 3. term, 4. cool

Continued on the next page…

No. Text title	Topic	Answers
21. DVD Review:	Initials and acronyms	PG, or UFO or LCD liquid crystal display, RAAF
22. Storm Surges:	Prefixes: micro and macro	a minute (small) life form, kangaroo or wallaby
23. Fjords and Sounds:	Pesky prepositions 1	1. between, 2. of, 3. off, 4. among
24. The Dogman:	Being precise: laugh/cry words	Examples: giggled, grinned, chuckled, smiled, beamed
25. Artist Interview:	Person for pronouns	1. (2, 3, 3), 2. (2, 1), 3. first, 4. second
26. Common and Proper Nouns:	Eponyms and toponyms	See table below. (Note: responses may vary)

Proper noun	Common noun	Meaning	Source
Afghan	afghan	woollen shawl style used in Afghanistan	place
Diesel	diesel	fuel for motors	inventor
Vandal	vandal	destroyer of property	Germanic race
Atlas	atlas	book of maps	Greek myth
Aurora	aurora	lights seen above the North/South poles	goddess of dawn
China	china	tableware – crockery	place of origin
Scrooge	scrooge	miserly person – a Dickens character	literature

No. Text title	Topic	Answers
27. How to Cope with Phishing:	Usage: similar to / different from	1. from, 2. to
28. Emergency Exit Plan:	Plurals for acronyms/initials	1. IMBs, 2. PINs, 1970s
29. Lady in Black:	Adding ing to -ic words	trafficking, politicking, panicking,
30. Bubonic Plague:	Correct usage: opposite	1. noun, 2. adjective
31. Cua Van Village:	Commas in series	(One comma only needed.)

Uncles and aunts, nieces and nephews and close neighbours went to the fair.

No. Text title	Topic	Answers
32. Twilight Walk:	Should of/have	Oral responses
33. Tales of a Fourth Grade Nothing:	Apostrophes for plurals	mice's tails, Dad's hat, babies' milk, women's meeting, boys' class
34. The Cathedral Fig:	Hyphens	X-ray, top-notch, father-in-law, sugar-free, fifty-five, 4-bedroom flat
35. Janus Words:	Onomatopoeia	electric motors hum, car horns toot
36. Mt Hypipamee Crater:	Correct usage	1. From 2. for
37. Piano Keys:	Characters' names	Examples: Henry, Bertha: Zack, Liam
38. Bellbirds:	Italics	1. *Frankenstein*, 2. *funny/furry*, 3. *Homo sapiens*, 4. *whole (or ate)*
39. Eyre's Journey:	o' words	lash (whip), Scottish cap
40. Bon Voyage:	Correct words	1. has to, 2. going to, 3. because, 4. are not, 5. his

Understanding Year 6 Comprehension
A. Horsfield © Five Senses Education © W. Marlin

Notes